EFFECTIVE
CLASSROOM
CONTROL

EFFECTIVE CLASSROOM CONTROL

Understanding Teacher–Pupil Relationships

Second edition

JOHN ROBERTSON
Homerton College, Cambridge

Edited by

Denis Lawton, B.A., Ph.D.
Professor of Education and Director,
University of London Institute of Education

HODDER AND STOUGHTON
LONDON SYDNEY AUCKLAND TORONTO

The male pronoun 'he' is mainly used in this book in the generic sense to apply to both male and female. This is simply to avoid tortuous constructions such as the following, which occurred in a recent publication: '. . . in which his/her perception of him/herself and of other people is distorted by his/her previous experiences.'

First published 1981
Second Edition 1989
Second impression 1990

Copyright © 1989 John Robertson

British Library Cataloguing in Publication Data

Robertson, John, *1937–*
  Effective classroom control.——2nd ed.
  1. Schools. Classrooms. Discipline——
  For teaching
  I. Title II. Lawton, Denis, *1931–*
371.1′024

ISBN 0–340–50508–7

Printed in Great Britain for Hodder and Stoughton Educational, a division of Hodder and Stoughton Limited, Mill Road, Dunton Green, Sevenoaks, Kent by St Edmundsbury Press Ltd, Bury St Edmunds, Suffolk.

Contents

Acknowledgments

I should like to express my thanks to the many students and teachers who have allowed me to observe and video-tape their teaching and who have discussed with me the views offered in this book. I am also grateful to Sean Neill of the University of Warwick with whom I have shared materials and ideas; to Jo Foweraker of Hodder and Stoughton for her careful editing and to Wendy Polito for typing the revised manuscript.

John Robertson

To Ashling, Rowan and Romneya

Introduction

I once overheard a headmaster remarking to a friend at a conference that he couldn't understand how a 'slip of a girl' on his staff should have no difficulty in controlling her classes, whereas a hefty male colleague was like putty in their hands. This book attempts to provide some explanations for this paradox. It is usually the case that difficult pupils only present extreme problems for some members of staff, whereas others seem to be able to cope with them fairly easily. The approach adopted in the following chapters is, therefore, 'teacher-centred'. Rather than being primarily concerned with why certain children are more disruptive than others, an attempt is made to explain why some teachers experience less difficulty than others in managing their classes.

We must perhaps acknowledge that a normal day school may not be the most appropriate educational setting for those pupils who create difficulties for even the most experienced of staff. However, research into coping with emotionally disturbed children in normal schools suggests that they respond to techniques of good classroom management in the same way as non-disturbed children (Kounin and Obradovic 1968). It may seem to some readers that to focus on the problems facing teachers is somewhat callous. Should we not concentrate on the problems facing the individual child, problems which explain why he needs to behave as he does? This approach has certainly not been neglected; indeed, there is a wealth of literature concerning early experiences, learning difficulties and emotional maladjustment in children. These factors are referred to in Chapter 5, but no attempt is made to provide a comprehensive description of the association between environmental factors and behaviour problems. Such an approach usually offers little to the teacher by way of practical advice in classroom management, though it may have wider implications for social and educational changes. The questions most teachers are concerned with are how to reduce the unwanted behaviour and how to deal effectively with it when it occurs, and this book aims to offer practical advice in these respects.

Unfortunately, the use of the word 'control' offends some teachers, as it smacks of an authoritarian regime which denies children any rights or respect. Nevertheless it is often a more appropriate term than alternatives such as 'management' or 'discipline', as the context is frequently one of controlling communication and interactions as well as one's own responses. It will become clear that there are no authoritarian connotations intended by using the term, as the emphasis is largely on understanding the nature of authority in teacher-pupil relationships with the aim of avoiding, if possible, the need to force pupils to comply with the demands made on them. There is an attempt to clarify what is entailed in maintaining cooperative relationships based on the teacher's authority so that conditions can be established in which learning can take place. Children are not the victims of classroom control, they are the beneficiaries. Furthermore, without their cooperation classroom control is not possible – as with any relationship both partners must work to maintain it.

In the past ten years there has been a rapid growth in the number of articles and books devoted to various aspects of classroom discipline and disruptive behaviour and some of the more relevant findings have been included. A rigorous and exhaustive analysis has been avoided in favour of offering the reader some coherent, practical advice although, naturally, only the teacher can decide if any particular course of action is appropriate. Special attention is given to the hidden messages conveyed in non-verbal and verbal communication. Gestures, vocal variations, facial expressions and other bodily movements can reveal a teacher's insecurity or boredom, his confidence or enthusiasm. Unlike words, their meaning is often ambiguous and can only be interpreted reliably if we have other information, such as the status of the speaker and what he is saying. Nevertheless, when there is any discrepancy between the meaning of the words being spoken and the non-verbal behaviour accompanying them, it is the latter which we take to reveal the true feelings of the speaker. For example, we know whether we are really welcome when we call unexpectedly on a friend, regardless of what is actually said. When non-verbal behaviour is consistent with the meaning of the words used, it may even pass unnoticed, though its message will still be received by the listener. Non-verbal communication and language also feature strongly in the expression of authority and power but, surprisingly, there have been few attempts to describe their role in detail in practical situations such as teaching. This will be a major focus throughout the book as it is essential that teachers understand the way they exchange unspoken messages with pupils.

Rather than present a series of theoretical perspectives and attempt to show their educational relevance, the opposite approach has been taken. Illustrations and transcripts taken from video and audio-taped lessons are presented, which hopefully all teachers will be familiar with, and interpretations of the significant features of the interaction are offered.

Non-verbal behaviours, in the form of the actions we carry out, are particularly significant in the expression of status and power and the first chapter considers this in some detail. Various features of behaviour are illustrated and the underlying messages about relationships being claimed are discussed. The second chapter gathers together the points established and attempts to describe the process whereby authority is negotiated and how it is affected when teachers use persuasion or resort to power. The view developed in the first chapter is that teachers who wish to establish their authority should behave as if they were already *in* authority. This is not as simple or as obvious as it sounds. A teacher, by virtue of his higher status, has certain rights to behave in ways denied to pupils, and in exercising those rights he reinforces his authority. This does not mean that he should be repressive or authoritarian, but rather that his behaviour should be consistent with his status. Pupils are less likely to question a teacher's authority if, by his behaviour, he defines the situation as one in which his authority is legitimate. It is particularly important for a teacher to do this in the first meetings with a new class, and it is mainly within this context that ways of conveying status are discussed in the third chapter.

The major bases for legitimacy, as far as teachers' long-term authority is concerned, are not simply the ascribed powers and institutional status but more the personal qualities they possess which contribute to their effectiveness as teachers. In this respect, Chapter 4 considers the role of non-verbal behaviour in sustaining pupils' attention and controlling the emotional climate of the classroom.

Chapter 5 presents an analysis of unwanted behaviour based on three different perspectives. These have been chosen to help teachers understand why some children are prone to misbehave and what can be done to reduce the opportunities and encouragements for them to do so. The first two perspectives consider the causes and rewards for un-wanted behaviour and the third perspective deals with various aspects of classroom management, including the role of questioning. Proficiency in this aspect of teaching contributes to the legitimacy of the teacher's claim to be in authority. There is clearly a close link between preventing unwanted behaviour and dealing effectively with it, and the emphasis in the first five chapters is mainly on creating conditions in which it is least likely to occur. However, prevention is not always possible and Chapter 6 considers the various ways in which teachers can respond when it does occur, and the implications these have for the authority agreement with pupils.

In the final chapter, some ways are suggested in which teachers can help one another to improve or better understand the techniques of good teaching and classroom control. To assist in this process a checklist of behaviours associated with various aspects of teaching is presented (p.150). This checklist is indexed to the main text to facilitate reference on specific problems and enhance the practical value of the book.

It is hoped that this book will give experienced teachers a greater insight into situations with which they may already be familiar, and that less experienced teachers and student teachers – who are frequently very concerned about classroom control – may begin to recognise some of the reasons why difficulties arise.

1 Expressing Authority

This chapter looks at aspects of our behaviour which characterise authority relationships and it is important to explain some of the distinctions which will be made. Mehrabian (1972) carried out research on how status differences are conveyed and the two dimensions of bodily behaviour which he identified will be referred to in the subsequent discussion.

The first dimension, which he termed *immediacy*, includes those behaviours which 'increase the mutual sensory stimulation between two persons'. To put this another way, immediacy behaviours tend to focus or intensify communication between people, so that they have greater impact on each other. Included in this dimension would be touching, closer position, forward lean, eye contact and more direct body orientation. Immediacy behaviours seem to be particularly involved in communicating the extent that one person likes or feels aggressive towards another. The second dimension, which is involved in the communication of status, Mehrabian termed *relaxation*, as evidenced by bodily posture. Relaxation is conveyed by an asymmetrical positioning of the limbs, openness of arm position, a sideways lean and tilt of the head or, if the speaker is seated, a more reclined position.

In any hierarchical organisation some members have different degrees of status and for the purpose of this discussion they will be referred to as *superiors* and *subordinates*. In school, a teacher may be a superior in his status relationship with a pupil, but a subordinate with the headteacher. In some cases, authority relationships may operate between pupils, even though they are nominally of the same status, by virtue of particular attributes which one possesses and others value. Some readers may find the terms offensive because of other connotations they have, but they will be used here only to denote differences in 'rank' or to label any behaviour which expresses status differences. A more neutral term, instead of 'superior', would be 'superordinate' but this is less familiar and rather cumbersome.

Argyle (1975) stated that 'Dominance relationships occur when there are no clear differences of power or status between people. Dominance signals are used to establish status differences where there is no objective basis for such differences, as in groups of primates'. It could be argued that there are clear and objective differences of power and status between pupils and teachers, so that dominance behaviour need never arise. Teachers are not only adults, but they also have ascribed powers over pupils. This may have made a difference in times gone by, when children 'knew their place', but is of little consequence now, and each teacher must establish his own authority. One exception may be in shared teaching situations where children transfer appropriate behaviour to the weaker members of a teaching team in the presence of a stronger teacher. Unfortunately, there are many occasions when the teacher's authority is not accepted. For example, a pupil may refuse to comply with an instruction and it is at times such as these that dominant behaviour may be observed. This 'show of force' to assert one's status, and any submissive behaviour which results, differ markedly from the way people behave when status differences are accepted in the relationship. A superior does not have to show dominant behaviour if his status is accepted; a subordinate need not show submissive behaviour unless he is threatened.

Argyle's use of the term 'dominance relationship' is not helpful in this discussion as regular dominant and submissive displays are a feature of interactions where the status relationship is in dispute. Once this is settled, the status relationship may be maintained on the basis of the power of the superior to make the subordinate comply (see p.30). In this sense, the term 'power relationship' might be a better description as dominant and submissive behaviour only occurs on those occasions when disputes over status arise.

Dominant behaviour is largely conveyed by postural cues, tone of voice and facial expression, and probably implies an element of threat through increased immediacy and tension demonstrated by a lack of movement when speaking (see p.71). Such behaviour might be judged as firm or resolute, but it can easily escalate perilously into an actual threat using a frown and a 'You'd better do as I say or else' tone of voice. The threat need not be stated verbally, though it often is, as will be discussed later. A more animated display, such as pointing or stabbing at the addressee, shouting and speaking rapidly in a higher pitched voice, may be perceived as threatening, being associated with anger and signalling imminent physical assault. However, in schools such displays can only be an alternative to physical assault, as it is illegal actually to strike children even as a formal punishment. An animated display of temper can therefore become a sign of frustration and impotence in the face of behaviour which the teacher is unable to control. In practice it is very unlikely that status differences in pupil-teacher relationships are maintained solely on the basis of power because, apart from the problems this may cause (see p.24), teachers do not have sufficient power over pupils to guarantee their compliance.

The distinction between high status and dominant behaviours will become clearer in the following discussion which considers how authority is expressed in different aspects of our interactions.

Posture

Mehrabian showed that when people of different status meet and talk, the lower status person adopts a more upright posture than the higher status person. It is interesting to speculate on the practical function of this difference. In Figure 1 the boy is being questioned by the teacher about his behaviour during the lesson. The pupil's relaxed, asymetrical posture and his studied unconcern are very characteristic expressions of resistance by those who do not wish to accept their subordinate position.

Figure 1 *'You completely wasted your time this lesson!'*

As Mehrabian pointed out, we tend to assume very relaxed postures with those we dislike or do not respect. Recently, a defendant in court was fined for lounging in the dock and having his hands in his pockets, which was seen by the magistrate as disrespectful. Teachers frequently attempt to 'correct' such postures by telling pupils to stand up straight and remove their hands from their pockets, not because pupils will thereby be able to hear more clearly, but to make them show respect for the status of the teacher. The occasion is thus being defined as a formal one where such courtesies must be observed. There is little doubt that most pupils realise they are being disrespectful when they adopt very relaxed postures and this is evident in the deliberate, grudging way they stand up straight when told to do so. The posture they eventually reach is usually far from upright. How teachers might deal with such situations depends on a variety of factors, and these are discussed later (p.48).

There are obviously implications for teachers, particularly during their first meetings with pupils when relationships are in the formative stage. A vigilant, tense and aggressive attitude, apart from conveying little enthusiasm for the subject taught, suggests insecurity, as if one is actually expecting to be challenged. On the other hand, a slightly bowed posture with feet together and hands clasped in front of the body or holding on to a book, as illustrated in Figure 2, conveys a rather weak, submissive attitude. In the first meetings with pupils neither a 'God help the first one who steps out of line' attitude, nor a 'Hello, I'm friendly please don't hurt me' approach will do much to communicate that the teacher is secure in his authority. A moderately relaxed posture and facial expression does not have such connotations. Ideally pupils should greet the new teacher in an attentive way, sitting upright and looking at him and, in some schools there is still the practice of standing when the teacher first enters the room which can be seen as a ritualised enactment of subordinate behaviour. Such an habitual act, however, may not indicate any real respect for the teacher's authority. The *way* the pupils rise to stand, the positions they adopt, and how attentively they behave when they resume their seats would portray the actual relationship. The fact that this practice has largely been abandoned is an expression of the increasing informality and egalitarianism between teachers and pupils and it is now usually reserved for occasions when the class is being noisy and inattentive and not responding to requests to be quiet. The teacher may then order the class to stand which serves to interrupt whatever they are doing (see p.32) and requires them to act as subordinates.

It seems, then, that status difference is conveyed more by the reactions of the lower status person than by the actions of the higher status person. An upright posture or a deliberately exaggerated relaxed posture acknowledges the higher status of the other, in the former case complying with it, and in the latter challenging it. There is an interesting example of a ritualised form of this behaviour in the Armed Services. Officers are permitted, or perhaps expected, to assume relatively relaxed

Figure 2 *'My name is Miss Jennings and I'm your new teacher.'*

positions when returning a salute, whereas other ranks must maintain erect postures. The command 'Attention' is very revealing, as it is used to instigate an upright and tense postural position, while also requiring attention in the cognitive sense. This is quite consistent with Mehrabian's findings, as the 'attention' posture is assumed in the presence of higher ranking officers, who can then decide whether to give permission to stand 'at ease'.

Figure 3   *'Put the date at the top of the page . . .'*

Because there is an association between an erect posture and signs of respect and attention, it might follow that a high degree of relaxation could be associated not only with a lack of respect, but also with a lack of attention. Mehrabian has shown this to be the case, and there are occasions when teachers unconsciously respond to such signals from pupils. If a boy is lounging in his seat when the teacher addresses the class, he may be told to 'sit up' or 'pay attention' if the teacher feels the pupil is not sufficiently alert.

I have asked teachers what their reaction would be if the Director of Education walked into the staffroom during a lunch hour. Most agreed that they would feel awkward if they were in very relaxed positions and would be inclined to adopt more upright postures, particularly if they were approached personally. Many teachers felt that it would be disrespectful not to show signs of alertness and attention in this situation, as a relaxed posture is associated with a more casual, informal attitude. It may be that the responsibility to give attention rests more with the lower status person on such occasions, while the higher status person can define the situation as he wishes, either by putting others at their ease with a remark like 'Please don't let me disturb you' or by allowing the formality of the interaction to continue. A subordinate is not expected to take such initiatives and most headteachers would be surprised if pupils entered their rooms and sat down without invitation. However, they themselves would probably stand if a visitor to the school came in, and they might even invite that person to be seated first, before they resumed their seats. Some headteachers I have discussed this with have argued that this is simply polite behaviour but the fact remains that *standing* is the postural action chosen to express politeness.

Orientation

In Figure 3 the teacher is explaining a piece of work to the pupil. If we did not know that these were the circumstances, are there any cues to suggest status difference between them? Is it significant that the teacher is holding the book whereas the pupil is standing passively and listening? Superiors may have to explain or give information to subordinates but the reverse is also true. One person is obviously younger than the other which makes it probable that he is of lower status but, could he in fact be a member of a Royal Family visiting the school? Some might argue that we naturally consider men to be of higher status than women in any occupational setting, though such gender stereotyping is rapidly disappearing. However, if we imagine the youth in Figure 3 to be a man, would this alter our impression of any status difference?

What is probably the most salient cue to the status difference is the fact that the woman is talking to the youth *without facing him* whereas he is facing her. Using Mehrabian's description, he is making his behaviour more *immediate* towards her, giving a direct body orientation and attending to her. The responsibility to give attention in this positional manner rests more with subordinates than superiors and if the reader is in any doubt about this, a number of variations of the above interaction could be acted with a colleague and others could be asked to judge which person appears to be of higher status. One could vary the person talking, holding the book, facing and so on as long as one avoided exaggerated postural and facial cues because these will affect interpretations. Figure 4 shows two teachers discussing a piece of work and their positioning is much more consistent with their status being equal.

It is obviously not the case that when they talk, pupils always face teachers and teachers never face pupils. What is proposed is that the positions adopted can give cues to the status relationship of the participants and to the formality of the occasion. The greater the status

Figure 4   *'How are we supposed to cover all this?'*

difference, or the more formal the meeting, the more likely it is that the subordinate will face the superior. He does not have the implied right to turn away when talking as readily as his superior. On some ceremonial occasions it is considered disrespectful to turn one's back to the 'leader' when leaving his presence and the subordinate is even expected to back out of the room.

In situations where pupils may be resisting the demands made on them, it is possible to observe them deliberately turning away in an unconcerned manner when a teacher is addressing them, as shown in Figure 5. This is often accompanied by a relaxed posture as described in the previous section. The pupil appears to be looking out of the window and does not seem interested in what is being said. There may also be

Figure 5 *'Why don't you bring your books to the lesson?'*

many other significant aspects of the pupil's behaviour in such situations such as giving short replies, talking in an exaggeratedly bored voice and disagreeing with whatever is being said, but the refusal to face is an important cue. This is evident when teachers attempt to assert their authority as they often demand 'Look at me when I'm talking to you!' as well as trying to get the pupil to stand or 'sit up straight'.

The postural cues described by Mehrabian's relaxation-tension dimension tend to be salient and override any positional cues as can be seen in Figure 6. The young girl appears to be in a position of superiority despite the conflicting cues of age, height, gender, body orientation and direction of gaze, simply because the man is standing 'to attention'.

Figure 6 *Which person is in authority?*

Figure 7 *'What do you think you're playing at, Sunshine?'*

When teachers are reprimanding pupils, they may sometimes face and even lean towards them (see Figure 7). The posture is usually tense and the manner clearly has aggressive overtones. Such behaviour is not an expression of higher status but an attempt by the teacher to *dominate* the pupil, to explicitly 'remind' him that he should show appropriate subordinate behaviour. It is more an expression of personal power (see p.45) and the pupil can be seen looking down which is usually taken to be a submissive response to such treatment.

Use of territory

Territorial rights are 'understood' in a wide range of species, not least human beings. The way we enter a room in our own house will differ from the way we enter an unfamiliar room, particularly if we expect to find someone of higher status than ourselves in there. It follows that an observer can infer the degree of status difference acknowledged or 'understood' by a person entering a room from the way he behaves. In Figure 8 the pupil is reluctant to enter fully into the room without being invited and this is quite typical of how some pupils enter a headteacher's room, particularly if they are new to the school. In my own school days, even to knock on the staffroom door took considerable courage and this was reinforced by the fact that very few pupils were ever permitted to enter. In any organisation which is hierarchically structured, subordinates probably feel similarly inhibited about entering the rooms of those in very high status positions. Having entered, they are more likely to stand and face the superior, whereas a superior might move around freely in a subordinate's room while holding a conversation.

The practice of making a class wait outside the classroom before the teacher arrives and gives permission for them to enter probably has territorial implications. There are clearly more obvious reasons concerning behaviour in an unsupervised room, or safety in a laboratory, but there is also an understanding that the teacher can deny entry and that pupils should enter in an orderly controlled manner. If they do not, they may be ordered to leave the room and the teacher will then control their re-entry. This can be construed as requiring the pupils to acknowledge the status of the person whose room they are entering. It is not their territory, but the teacher's. The significance of this aspect of our behaviour is highlighted by the rituals controlling entry into places of worship. When entering the presence of the Almighty one's behaviour must communicate more than respect.

Moving freely around the classroom will help to convey that it is one's own territory, although teachers will naturally use some regions more than others. In a conventionally arranged classroom, with the pupils in rows facing the front, the teacher's area would be at the front of the room, and if he seldom ventured among the pupils they would certainly notice it when he did. I remember one teacher when I was at school who would pace the gangways whenever we were working, clicking his heels as he walked. He only stopped in order to reprimand a pupil, never to praise; so as he approached, one could feel the tension mount as heads lowered and pens scribbled. He used our 'territory' with disdain and made his presence felt. Nowadays such behaviour would probably provoke a resentful response, as teachers tend to move among pupils more frequently and with less hostile intentions, particularly where tables are arranged in informal groupings and where pupils also have

Figure 8 *'Excuse me, Sir.'*

Figure 9 *'Don't forget to show all your working out.'*

freedom of movement around the room. Ideas of territory are still relevant, however, but are probably more concerned with the personal space immediately around one's body and personal territory such as one's seat or desk. In Figure 9 the teacher is casually sitting on the edge of the pupil's desk. Such relaxed behaviour is quite typical of teachers who prefer an informal atmosphere to prevail but, even they might feel uncomfortable if pupils perched on their desks while they were sitting at them. Similarly, if one pupil encroaches too far on another's part of the table he will probably be told to move, whether or not that space is being used. High status or 'important' people usually have a larger personal territory such as their own office rather than a shared one, and similarly their personal space is larger. This is most evident in the formal way in which members of Royal families are greeted. The initiative for approach is left to them, and the other person is expected to give a submissive greeting, such as bowing or curtseying, and should not initiate conversation. There is a less dramatic example of the same phenomenon in schools where the headteacher is usually given a private room (and sometimes toilet) and is less easily approached by teachers.

There are cultural differences in how close we expect others to approach us in normal conversation. For example, Watson and Graves (1966) found that Arab students adopted closer positions than American students. We can learn to modify our notions of what constitutes our personal space and in what circumstances others might enter it. The *intention* of the other is taken into account as we tolerate actual bodily contact in very crowded situations. Argyle (1975) points out that we avoid eye contact at such times, probably to reduce the intimacy of the closeness. If another person *intentionally* enters our personal space, particularly if they are facing and looking at us, it can be very arousing or stressful, and the motives for such action are usually affectionate or aggressive. Eye contact is particularly significant at such times and will be dealt with in a later section.

The manner in which one enters a pupil's personal space is, therefore, very important. At one extreme, facing and looking directly at, and if possible, down at the pupil is likely to induce considerable arousal and Weinraub and Putney (1978) have shown that babies as young as nine months are upset if an adult 'towers' over them. On the other hand, an indirect approach, looking at the pupil's work, not facing him directly and squatting down to his level, will be far less arousing and is unlikely to be perceived as directly threatening. If the pupil is young and unfamiliar, insecure or disturbed, such an approach would create less anxiety. Figures 19 and 20 (pp.36 and 37) contrast these two extremes, and in Figure 19 a teacher is shown bending down to talk in a comforting way to a partially-sighted girl. Even in this example there are probably still status implications as it would seem incongruous for a child to bend down in this manner to a seated teacher, the implication being that superiority has temporarily been foregone.

A sudden violation of personal space, particularly if unexpected, may be very stressful for the pupil. I observed one teacher who had warned an eleven-year-old boy on several occasions to stop talking and get on with his work. The boy was talking yet again and disturbing his neighbour, so the teacher, who was attending to someone at the back of the room, approached quietly from behind. Simultaneously she put her hand on his left shoulder and leant to within six inches of his left ear saying, 'Now take your books and work at the front'. The boy was half out of his seat before she had finished her sentence and had to be reminded to take his books. Though she had not used a threatening tone or shouted, the close proximity and surprise of her behaviour caused an immediate response. Touching the pupil was also an expression of status, and will be dealt with later.

Teachers frequently move nearer to pupils they suspect are not attending, which usually has the desired effect and there is evidence that

Figure 10   *'You should be listening, not writing.'*

other aspects of their performance, such as listening comprehension, also improve. Smith (1979), in a summary of such research, concluded, '... the results are consistent with a number of other observations concerning the effects of teacher-student interpersonal distance: the closer the teacher is to the target group, the more effective he or she is according to some measure of student performance.'

Any layout of furniture which restricts the teacher from moving into the pupils' personal spaces may therefore, in some circumstances, limit the capacity to maintain their attention. In many informally arranged classrooms some pupils do not face the teacher and it would be interesting to discover whether there are any associated deficits in attention, though for much of the time they would probably be working independently or in small groups. A study carried out in a special school with a group of pupils aged between twelve and fifteen showed that for academic work there was a marked increase in on-task behaviour, from thirty-five per cent to seventy per cent, when children were arranged in rows rather than grouped around tables (Wheldall and Lam, 1987). Previous work has shown similar results with primary school children. The seating arrangements clearly have implications for pupil behaviour and may be related not only to interaction with and distraction from peers, but also to the extent that the teacher is able to make his presence salient for all the pupils.

The extent that differing territorial rights are observed between teachers and pupils gives expression to how they regard their status relationship. It is as much the avoidance of the superior's territory by the subordinate as it is the use of the subordinate's territory and personal space by the superior, that expresses these understandings. As with posture and bodily orientation it can be seen that the subordinate is not expected to reciprocate certain actions from the superior. The implication may be that the differential rights in some way *represent* or even constitute the status differences and without them there would be *de facto* equality. Further examples of differential rights can be seen in other aspects of teacher-pupil interaction.

Rights to property

A teacher is reading aloud to an attentive class who are following the story from their books. She notices that one girl is writing instead of following the story and Figure 10 shows her taking the pen from the girl's hand, which she then places on the desk before closing the exercise book in which the girl had been writing. The right to interrupt others' activities and to remove their property is one which teachers frequently exercise towards pupils. It is so common that when I show video-taped extracts of it happening, many teachers fail to notice it or, more accurately, to realise that it enacts the status relationship between the teacher and pupil. A teacher told me of when he was a pupil in the sixth form and had arrived late one morning. The teacher came over with the dinner register and told him that he had forgotten to sign it. 'I was half asleep at the time, so I just took the pen out of his hand to sign the register, and he clipped me round the head.'

It is quite surprising for teachers to have property removed from their hands by pupils and the act would be considered ill-mannered and disrespectful. If one wishes to borrow something from a superior it is appropriate to ask politely and wait hopefully for the article to be handed over. Where there is a great difference in status one might be reluctant even to ask. On the other hand it would not seem unusual for a superior to ask politely to borrow something, *while in the act of reaching for it.*

There are undoubtedly differential rights in relation to property and if these rights are questioned by the subordinate, it is the authority which they express which is in question. This is evident in situations where the teacher has 'lost control' of a class; if one attempted to interrupt a pupil by removing her property she might object and would probably pick up the pen again and continue to write. Naturally, if the pupil also considered herself to be in the right this would increase her resistance to the teacher's action, but how she perceived the difference in status, or wanted the teacher to perceive it, would similarly affect her response. I saw a young student teacher hold out her hand, indicating to an eight-year-old boy that he should give her his ruler as he had just been giving an impromptu recital on it. Instead of handing it to her he hid it behind his back and there followed a short bout of all-in wrestling before the student emerged triumphantly holding the ruler. The pupil had questioned the student's right to take the ruler but, by winning it in a fair fight, the student had behaved more like another pupil than a teacher. Had she remained with her hand outstretched, this would have implied that the boy did not have the option of refusing.

A measure of the extent to which pupils accept a teacher's authority can be seen by, at one extreme, blunt refusals to hand over what might actually be school property, to the other, where they will readily surrender money, watches or other valuable personal property for confiscation by the teacher. A close examination of video-tapes of such events will frequently show that the pupil actually hands over the offending object as the teacher reaches to remove it.

An attempt by a teacher to exercise differential rights in relation to property can be thought of as a *claim* to be in authority, implicitly stating that the action is legitimate. If the pupil complies, this will validate the claim and reinforce the teacher's authority whereas objecting will bring the authority into question. This interpretation, of course, also applies to the other expressions of status difference that have been discussed so far. Our behaviour does not *cause* others to act in accordance with our wishes. How they already perceive their relationship to us, particularly in respect of status, will affect their response.

Touching

There has been a great deal of research and observation devoted to the act of touching and though it is not possible to deal in depth with the subject here, it is important to consider how it may feature in the expression of status relationships.

Figure 11 *'Are you sure Mrs Brown said you could stay in?'*

There is nothing unusual in Figure 11 which shows a headteacher holding a pupil by the upper arm as he talks to him. What would seem strange is if the pupil were holding the headteacher by the arm. This unilateral right to touch is an expression of the status relationship between teachers and pupils. There are several qualifications one would have to make regarding this observation. People differ in the extent that they normally touch others. Some teachers rarely touch pupils and when they do so, seem to exercise a hygienic care usually reserved for dealing with contagious materials as shown in Figure 12 where the teacher is using a pencil to raise the head of a boy to whom he wishes to talk. Such

Figure 12 *'What do you call that scrawl?'*

disdainful treatment makes a claim to a considerable difference in power in the relationship, as it is difficult to imagine a situation where an adult would not feel very resentful unless it were done jokingly by a friend.

It is not unusual to observe a teacher adjusting a pupil's clothes during a conversation, perhaps straightening a collar or tie. In Figure 13 the pupil is receiving a mild reprimand and the teacher has previously lifted the pupil's hand from his pocket. As has already been discussed in this chapter, the teacher's less immediate orientation and more relaxed posture are quite consistent with the expression of higher status and, in

Figure 13 *'But you know what will happen if I catch you fooling around again.'*

adjusting the boy's shirt collar without comment or permission, he shows a mixture of patronising care and correction which can only be exercised by superiors. In passively accepting this treatment the pupil validates the teacher's definition of the situation.

In the examples chosen so far it has been intentional to show male teachers touching male pupils, as the relative sex and age of the people concerned affects the significance of the act. I have asked numerous groups of teachers whether they make any distinction between boys and girls when touching pupils and at the primary level it is unusual for a teacher to consider the sex of the pupil. However at secondary level, male teachers rarely admit to touching girls, presumably because of the possible sexual connotations. They may even have been advised not to remain alone in a room with a female pupil. Female secondary teachers do not usually make this distinction though some, particularly the younger ones, say they avoid touching older boys and it may be that the earlier onset of puberty in girls is a factor influencing this difference. Whether this has always been so, or whether it is the result of the present emphasis on sexual harassment by men, women are generally freer to touch men 'incidentally' than vice versa even when the men are of higher status. The act is unlikely to be construed as a sexual gesture or at least not one to which a man is expected to object and it may be that women are thus able to exercise a form of personal power in the interaction.

The 'intensity' of the touch, as well as the part of the body touched are other factors which bear upon the significance of the act. Resting a hand on another person's arm is less arousing for them than gripping their arm; touching a shoulder is less arousing than touching a leg. Primary school children are frequently touched on the head or have their hands held by teachers in caring and comforting ways as in Figure 14 where a new boy is being introduced by the headteacher to his teacher. The comforting hand on the back of his head is repeated by the teacher when she directs him to his seat (see Figure 15). Touching the head and holding pupils' hands is seldom seen in secondary schools except with the youngest classes, though one might anticipate that any pupil with special needs or obviously in need of some comfort might receive such treatment. Among adults, normally only those on mutually intimate terms hold hands or touch each other's heads unless one is in considerable distress, as such acts would seem extremely patronising from a superior.

In any conflict or confrontation, touch is likely to be perceived as aggressive, particularly if it is intense or abrupt. Some research by Neill (1987) has shown that boys and girls greatly dislike being touched in an angry manner and teachers should be aware that they may react violently. Even the threat to use physical force, perhaps to move a pupil from his seat, will often escalate a situation. Teachers need considerable social skills or confidence in their status relationship with pupils to risk touching them during a confrontation, as it is very easy to misjudge the response.

Figure 14 *'Can you make Robert at home in your class, Mrs Wilson?'*

Figure 15 *'Now you can sit over here with James.'*

Differences in personal style, age, sex, manner of touch, area touched and situation all affect the signficance of the act of touching, but the fact remains that when people feel they do not have the right to reciprocate they are acknowledging their subordinate position. This is likely to be the case in any hierarchical situation, so that it would be less likely for pupils to touch their teachers, teachers their headteachers, nurses their matrons, privates their sergeants and so on, than vice versa. Subordinates are not expected to touch their superiors except in strictly defined formal rituals such as handshaking when greeting, and if they do, it indicates a degree of informality which has transcended the status difference between them. Very young infants frequently treat the teacher like a parent and actively seek physical contact. Some pupils will tap a teacher on the arm to get attention but if pupils feel free to touch the teacher incidentally, this indicates a very informal relationship where the difference in status may be limited to specific occasions.

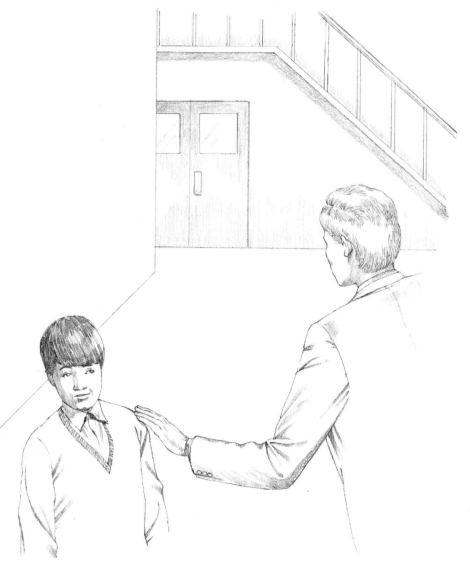

Figure 16 *'Off you go, then.'*

In Figure 16 the head teacher is 'directing' the pupil as he says 'Off you go then', an action which teachers frequently use towards pupils.

The fact that the headteacher is not even looking at the pupil contributes to the implication that the pupil will naturally follow the instruction and not object. Should a pupil resist physical direction, it would not be sensible to resort to force. It is not the *act* of resistance which the teacher would be dealing with, but *what the act implied about the relationship*. If the teacher 'wins' by force or threats, this implies that the basis for the authority is physical power; pupils comply with teachers' demands because they can be *made to comply*. It seems more appropriate to question the pupil with an attitude of disbelief, to ascertain what reason could possibly have prompted him to take such a step. In so doing, one implies that pupils should normally *grant* such rights to teachers.

The role of eye contact

Eye contact plays a very significant role in all interpersonal communication, providing those concerned with information about each other's intentions and feelings. It is particularly important in the communication of 'power and preference' (Exline, 1972) and, in this respect, it is useful for teachers to be aware of its role in their interactions with pupils. As with all non-verbal behaviour, but particularly so with eye contact, a reliable interpretation is only possible if given wider information about other relevant behaviour and the context in which it occurs.

When two people look at one another it usually follows that an interaction will take place. This could be in the form of a brief nod or acknowledgment, or they may begin to speak. It has already been noted that lower status is expressed by a more direct body orientation and it follows that subordinates have been observed to look more at superiors than vice versa, though they may usually be the first to look away (Strongman and Champness, 1968). Looking at the person who is speaking to you is a clear sign of attention. If eye contact is established between people and they do not speak, they usually quickly look away because to continue looking without speaking has particular significance in communication. As Exline suggests, gazing or staring at each other happens most frequently between those who are in conflict or attracted to one another. In conflict situations it usually represents an attempt to dominate the other, so it occurs where status differences have yet to be established or are in question. Boxers frequently try to gain a psychological advantage by 'staring-out' their opponents before the fight but not after the contest has been decided. To avert one's gaze first, particularly with a downward glance, is a submissive signal. As anyone who has engaged in a staring-out encounter will verify, it can be quite stressful and the one who looks away has probably found it necessary to relieve the tension. When very young children are introduced to a stranger they sometimes look down and cover their eyes with their hands and it may be that the downward glance of adults has its origin in this behaviour. In

Figure 17 the teacher had warned the boy that he would be kept in at lunchtime and the boy had exclaimed loudly, 'You what!' The teacher reacted by looking at, and moving towards him and the boy can be seen having lowered his head and shielding his eyes in a similar way to a young child under stress.

Figure 17   *'**What** did you say?'*

There is even evidence to show that such signals may operate between species, at least between humans and rhesus macaques (Exline and Yellin, 1969). In the study, it was possible to elicit threat behaviour or flight from a monkey by giving a challenging stare, whereas a deferential, downcast glance after preliminary eye contact had been established would forestall such responses. Averting the gaze in other directions does not seem to have the same significance, but the downward glance appears to be a fairly universal sign of submissive behaviour. This does not imply that teachers should be silently scanning the class, trying to stare out any pupil who cares to take up the challenge but should they chance to meet a pupil's gaze, sustaining eye contact in a relaxed way is likely to give an impression of confidence. This is particularly important when teachers first meet their classes and are likely to be the centre of attention. It is usually only a matter of seconds before a pupil will withdraw from a chance visual encounter (though it may seem like an eternity) but should this not happen, the situation can be 'rationalised' by asking the pupil a question, an act itself not devoid of status implications. A relaxed manner is crucial in mitigating the effects of prolonged gaze and moving closer, as any hint of bodily tension or menace in the facial expression is unambiguously threatening. One may thereby be committed to a confrontation with a determined pupil, without leaving the option of a graceful withdrawal (see p.138). It is in such apparently trivial ways that the teacher can build up the impression of security and confidence.

If, when someone is speaking, the listener intentionally withholds or withdraws eye contact, this can have an entirely different significance. Argyle and Cook (1976) point out that if a higher status person is reprimanding a lower status person, he may exercise control over the direction of gaze. Children are told to 'Look at me when I'm talking to you', whereas a private in the army would be made to keep looking straight ahead regardless of the vitriolic sergeant screaming into his ear. The speaker must control gaze direction, because the listener might otherwise easily express a lack of interest by deliberately looking, and even facing, elsewhere, or by breaking visual contact in a non-deferential way, such as by letting the gaze slowly move upward and away from the speaker. Such signals convey that the listener's attention is wandering, and if they are carried out deliberately the behaviour is very disrespectful. Measures to control the listener's direction of gaze are aimed at preventing or curtailing such behaviour. Pupils can be very adept at shutting teachers off by withholding eye contact, as the following extract illustrates. A special needs teacher is talking to a fourteen-year-old girl about her work in other lessons:

Teacher: What are you going to do after you've finished the project on East Anglia?

Pupil: (*Looking 90° away from teacher, and scratching her back in an unconcerned manner* (see Figure 18)) I ain't gonna do it. It's boring.

Teacher: Why is it boring?
Pupil: (*Stops scratching but continues to look away*) Well I don't want to
            learn about that do I?
Teacher: Well, a lot of the produce of . . .

Figure 18 *'I ain't gonna do it. It's boring.'*

Pupil: (*Interrupts and shifts position so that she is turned 90° away from the teacher*) When I get a job they're not gonna want to know about farming and everything like that. (*Stands and turns back to teacher, and shuffles some papers.*)

Teacher: That's true.

Pupil: Makes you sick.

Teacher: (*Talking to pupil's back*) But it's general knowledge really, isn't it? East Anglia is . . .

Pupil: (*Interrupts and sits back to the 90° position*) No, I don't wanna know it. (*Turns around and looks at papers again but does not stand.*)

Teacher: What are the most useful subjects for you to do, Jill? What is the best one?

Pupil: (*Still looking away*) Typing and English.

Teacher: Typing?

Pupil: Yeah, but I never learned it.

Teacher: Why not?

Pupil: Don't like the teacher, do I?

Teacher: No, I know you don't. What about your other subjects, Jill? Art? English?

Both speak together

Pupil: No I don't like them.

Teacher: What about Child Development?

Teacher   (*Continues*) Do you go to that?

Pupil: Sometimes.

Teacher: Because that's a practical subject. (*Pupil continues to look away in a bored manner, then looks towards, but not at, the teacher for the first time in the interaction, brushes hair from face with hand and looks down.*)

Teacher: (*Continues*) Are you still going out with Geoff?

Pupil: (*Glances at teacher and smiles*) Yeah.

Teacher: (*Laughs*).

Throughout the interview the pupil replied in a bored tone of voice and most of her comments were negative, clearly giving the impression that she had no interest in the conversation. She also interrupted the teacher on two occasions which did not acknowledge any status difference in the teacher's favour. Although she said that English was a useful subject she denied liking it when the teacher mentioned it a few seconds later. For most of the interview not only did the pupil withhold eye contact, but she also faced away from the teacher (see p.7). Only when the teacher stopped discussing work and spoke about her boyfriend did she deign to glance back and smile. In contrast, the teacher looked continuously at the pupil and spoke in a reasonable, sympathetic manner. Exline (1972) compared 'control oriented' subjects – those who described themselves as wishing to control others – with 'low control oriented' subjects, when faced with a listener who either looked at them all the time or 'never looked at all but swept the air above their heads'. He found that the low control oriented subjects looked more if the listener withheld his gaze, whereas the high control oriented subjects looked less. The interpretation suggested was that those who like to control others may find people whose visual attentions they cannot capture more powerful than those they can. Presumably such perceived power would not be so disconcerting for someone who was less inclined to exercise control.

The teacher in the above example is clearly not behaving in the manner of Exline's 'control oriented' subjects and some may consider this entirely appropriate in the context of a fairly informal chat with a pupil. However, in choosing not to look and resisting the teacher's attempt to gain her attention, the pupil seems able to exercise some control over the communication and the teacher may subsequently have found it difficult to relate to the girl on other than her terms, as it is also the relationship which is being enacted in this discussion about school work.

Eye contact, in conjunction with other aspects of our behaviour, is very significant in communicating our attitudes. The more intimate the subject being discussed or the closer that people stand, the more likely that one or both participants will look away, unless they mutually wish to increase the intimacy of their relationship. If a pupil is unable to look back in the face of an accusation it may appear as if he has something to hide, whereas an 'open', relaxed return of gaze gives an impression of truthfulness. It is suggested that cultural differences may lead to misunderstandings in these situations as some groups may have learned not to return the gaze of a superior, and it is therefore essential to consider the full range of non-verbal behaviour rather than to form an impression on the basis of any one signal. Nevertheless, patterns of eye contact can be very significant in the communication of intimacy, status and attempts to establish dominance, and teachers should be aware of the dilemma described by Exline: 'To look or not to look, that is the question'.

Who responds to whom?

Another finding quoted by Exline is that at the start of a conversation it is the dominant person who is the first to look away and immediately begin to speak. When differences in status are understood, those who believe themselves to be subordinates are more reluctant or inhibited about initiating an interaction than those who believe they are superior. By seizing the initiative to speak, a person may thereby be attempting to dominate the other by placing them in the position of having to respond. A *response* is not only a verbal reply but includes a wide variety of non-verbal behaviour, such as returning eye contact, showing anger, amusement or other feelings, and even a physiological reaction such as blushing, provided there is a *stimulus* of some sort. Similarly, if a stimulus interrupts a particular behaviour, the discontinuation of that behaviour would be regarded as a response to the stimulus. For example, if a pupil was about to talk to his friend, but was pre-empted by the teacher, the pupil's silence would be regarded as a response, whether or not he looked at the teacher.

Hargreaves (1972), in discussing discipline, points out that 'most experienced teachers insist that the teacher must, if he is to survive, define the situation in his own terms at once'. In the first meetings with pupils the status of the teacher is likely to be in question and it might be important to present oneself as one who initiates interactions rather than one who responds to the pupils' cues. The high status person in an interaction is able to exercise a good deal of control over the other's responses and, if status is in question, the one who exercises control will assume dominance. If a new teacher walks into a class and immediately begins to answer questions about himself in a friendly way, before he has addressed or made any impact on the whole class, it may seem unimportant, but it will certainly do nothing to establish his authority. An example of such an interaction with a group of twelve-year-olds, say, might proceed as follows:

> The teacher, on entering the room, looks at the pupils and returns a smile from a boy in the front. The boy continues to smile and asks a question:
>
> *1st Pupil:* Are you our new teacher, Miss?
> *Teacher:* (*Continuing to smile*) That's right. (*Another pupil calls out.*)
> *2nd Pupil:* Are you strict like Mr Brown was, Miss? (*Teacher looks towards him, takes a breath to answer, but another boy calls out to the previous pupil.*)
> *3rd Pupil:* He was a nut case! (*Laughter from class.*)
> *Teacher:* (*No longer smiling, looking at new speaker*) Now . . . that will do. I'd like your attention, please.

Such a sequence might last no more than fifteen seconds but would be very important. It began with one pupil giving a social signal, a smile, to the teacher, to which she responded appropriately. The pupil then asked a question which the teacher answered. This was closely followed by another question which the teacher was about to answer, but she was interrupted by another pupil. She responded by giving eye contact. There was laughter, to which she responded by giving a mild reprimand.

This example may seem harmless enough but, if this pattern of interaction were to continue, the teacher would soon find it difficult to retain any control over communication in the room. Her first objective should have been to get the whole class attending as quickly as possible, but instead the pupils were beginning to control her behaviour.

Mehrabian suggests that, in awkward or formal situations, smiling is associated with a communicator's effort to relieve tension and placate his addressee, and so has submissive connotations. The first smiles given to a new teacher could well be attempts to establish social contact, and thereby reduce or avoid any possible tension produced by the appearance of a stranger. If the teacher returns the smiles, this puts the pupils at ease, and this might not always be desirable on first meetings –

as suggested by the title of Kevin Ryan's book about probationary teachers, *Don't Smile till Christmas.*

The questions asked by the pupils in the above example probably had a function similar to smiling in that they were attempts to initiate social contact. Their underlying meaning was more in the nature of 'Hello I'm friendly, are you?' or 'Look at me, I'm the clown of the class!' If the teacher answers such questions or otherwise responds appropriately, the pupils are again put at their ease. This may, of course, in some situations be exactly what the teacher wishes to do. However, it is an important feature of classroom management that the teacher reserves the right to choose if and when she responds to pupils' questions (see p.105).

An entirely different impression would be created by a teacher who entered the room but did not return the pupil's smile. The boy would have been less inclined to follow with his question, 'Are you our new teacher, Miss?' If the teacher also chose to ignore this, and didn't look at the boy, but perhaps took up a prominent position in front of the class, the second pupil's remark would have seemed out of context. The atmosphere would not be that of friendly interchange because an element of tension had been generated by the teacher, and a pupil would need some courage and determination to call out. The simple act of choosing not to return a smile would appear enigmatic and maintain any tension in the meeting. However, should the teacher stare back coldly at any smiling pupil, the tension would be dangerously increased. By remaining unresponsive she would also have resisted accepting the pupil's definition of the situation. The teacher could then begin to define the situation in her own terms. She might, for example, walk over to a pupil, ask his name and tell him, in a friendly manner, to open a window. He would be unlikely to refuse and would thereby begin to validate the teacher's unstated claim to be the one who asks questions and gives instructions. The act of moving closer to a pupil, making one's behaviour more 'immediate' in Mehrabian's sense, would probably cause a physiological response from the pupil as well as imply the right to use his personal space (see p.12). By acting in accordance with the teacher's wishes in such apparently trivial and innocuous ways, it subsequently becomes more difficult for a pupil to alter this initial definition of the situation by refusing to comply when more onerous demands are made.

It is interesting to consider a parallel which can be drawn between the teacher facing a new class and an interrogation with a prisoner, a situation discussed by Danziger (1976). It goes without saying, of course, that the circumstances are very different. Interrogators have much more power over their prisoners than do teachers over pupils, and their intentions are very different. All that may be similar is that it is in the interests of both teachers and interrogators to define the situation in their own terms. Danziger describes how manuals of interrogation techniques 'stress the need to emphasise the power of the interrogator in many small ways, telling the prisoner where he may or may not sit, making it necessary for him to ask for permission to smoke, go to the washroom, have a drink of water, use the telephone, or rest'. The prisoner is clearly being denied any rights but Danziger goes on to point out the dangers of such a hostile presentation:

> But if the interrogator limited himself to displays of power he would run the risk of achieving exactly the opposite of what he is after with many prisoners. By these means he may merely confirm the prisoner's definition of the interrogator as the enemy who is to be defied. This is particularly likely to happen if the prisoner is a hardened criminal, an ideologically convinced opponent or a member of the other side in a war.

There are clearly implications here for the use of reprimands and punishments but in making any demands on pupils there is always the danger of provoking a belligerent response. Even in the harmless act of asking a pupil's name a hint of hostility will confirm to him that the teacher is 'the enemy who is to be defied' and he is just as likely to reply 'What's yours?' thereby throwing the responsibility to respond back on the teacher.

Faced with signs of resistance in the pupil, some teachers raise their voices or try to interrupt the first sign of an unwanted rejoinder in an attempt to retain the initiative in the interaction. However, there is little one can do when faced with a pupil determined to challenge one's authority, and such confrontations are better avoided, particularly in front of other pupils where neither teacher nor pupil wishes to lose face by backing down.

The reader who has never been at the mercy of a group of unruly children who pay no heed to demands or pleas, may feel that too much attention is being given to the first minutes of an interaction. Nevertheless, a great deal of research and observation has shown them to be very significant in the teacher's attempt to establish authority and they will be further considered later (p.50) as it is the outcomes of these interactions which will influence subsequent meetings. One hears of footballers being told to win the first tackle decisively, as this gives a psychological advantage over the opponent, and the teacher should also try to ensure that a potentially difficult class do not define the situation in their own terms at the outset. The experienced teacher will avoid bullying, shouting, sarcasm and other such methods, as these really only reveal one's own insecurity.

While supervising a student on a teaching practice, I once found myself involved in a potential confrontation with a pupil. The school was an urban comprehensive where the vast majority of the boys spend the winter days dressed in jeans and parkas. This gives a rather temporary atmosphere to the whole place, as if they won't take their coats off because they're not stopping. As I came down a flight of stairs during the break, I noticed that I had become the focus of attention for a group of fourteen-year-old boys lounging on a railing on the landing in front of me. I neither returned their stares nor avoided chance eye contact, but as I reached the landing one of them called out 'Hiya sir'. What he was really saying was something like 'Hello fat face', which was clearly conveyed by his sneering manner. Had I replied, 'Good morning', or even ignored the remark, he would have demonstrated to his friends his ability to be rude to adults and get away with it. Perhaps a liberal approach would have been to acknowledge his greeting and put any implied ridicule down to his immaturity, but I'm not sure whether that would have done either of us any good. Anyway, for some reason I wasn't in the mood to be an innocent victim, so I walked over to within a foot of him, looked him squarely in the face, and said in a relaxed way, 'I beg your pardon?'

Making one's behaviour very immediate for the addressee, but using a non-threatening tone and expression, makes one's feelings and intentions very ambiguous, and the boy would have been unsure how to interpret my action. He must have found my prompt non-verbal move quite unsettling, because he looked down, avoiding my gaze, and said, 'Nuffin'. There was a noticeable change in his tone, so I felt able to press on: 'Did you speak to me?' He looked up briefly, perhaps to check that my expression was not threatening, and replied quietly, 'Yeah'.

'What did you say?' I asked. He looked a little sheepish but found the courage to establish eye contact once again: 'I said, Hello.' I left a brief pause and replied, 'Good morning', then turned and walked away. Dominance in the interaction was achieved by avoiding a predictable response to the initial greeting, and then forcing the pupil to do all the responding. Had we met again he would probably have been more wary. It might, however, have been more sensible to have confirmed my friendliness, perhaps by asking him to direct me to my destination, rather than to score a point over him (see p.140).

By attention to such details from the very start of an interaction one can quickly establish control over communication. The extent and duration of this initial 'detached' approach will depend upon the willingness of the pupils to respond appropriately, but it will only be effective if the teacher can convey, by his non-verbal behaviour, that he is confident and at ease.

Forms of address

In Figure 19 a seven-year-old partially-sighted girl has arrived late, as the taxi bringing her got lost. It is her second day at the school, having spent her infant years in a special unit for the visually handicapped, so the teacher is being particularly attentive and caring towards her. This is evident from the hand placed round her shoulder and the way the teacher stoops down to talk to her: 'Have you got a reading book, Darling?'

The form of address chosen is in keeping with the caring attitude and is in stark contrast with the way the teacher speaks to another girl only a few seconds later, whom she discovers looking in a cupboard (see Figure 20) – 'And what are *you* doing here, Young Lady?' On this occasion the teacher remains standing and looks down on the child (see p.15). The forms of address chosen by the teacher in each case clearly express very different definitions of the situation. One child is in a caring relationship with a parent figure, the other in a formal subordinate relationship with an authority figure. The form of address we choose can, therefore,

Figure 19　*'Have you got a reading book, Darling?'*

Figure 20 *'And what are you doing here, Young Lady?'*

express how we wish the other person to understand the circumstances. These may only be temporary however (as in the example above) because when the partially-sighted girl has settled in and the incident of the cupboard has passed, the teacher would return to using christian names. In other special circumstances, such as some committee meetings or debating societies, we may be expected to use more formal forms of address which are adopted only on those occasions. Teachers may address one another formally in front of pupils but revert to first names in the staffroom.

Other factors influence the form of address we choose such as the degree of intimacy shared, that is how well we know one another, whether we are related in kinship and whether we are roughly of the same generation. It is also clear that status differences will be reflected in our choice, a fact summarised by Danziger (1976):

> Where there is a choice between a polite and a familiar form of the pronoun of address the inferior person generally uses the polite form to his superior and in turn receives the familiar form. In medieval Europe the master used the familiar form to the servant as did the nobility to commoners and parents to children; in return they expected to receive the polite form. But equals would use the same form to each other, and this might be either the polite or the familiar form. Thus the asymmetrical use of pronouns of address would be used to present the existence of a status differential in the relationship.

Familiar forms of pronouns of address, such as 'tu' in French or Italian, have largely fallen out of use in England though in some parts of the North, 'thee' and 'thou' can still be heard and children would not be expected to use this form towards adults and particularly teachers. There is evidence that this principle may be widespread in human societies, as Howell (1981) found that among the Chewong, a small aboriginal group in the rain forest of Peninsula Malaysia, it was disrespectful to address 'certain categories of affines' with the familiar form 'thou' or to behave in other intimate ways.

Teachers may address pupils by first names or even nicknames if they so choose, but pupils are not expected to reciprocate. In schools where they are permitted to, it expresses a more informal and equal relationship. In the earlier example, the use of 'darling' is quite consistent with this principle, as the pupil would be considered cheeky if she addressed the teacher thus but the use of 'young lady' is interesting. Teachers frequently use a variety of less 'familiar' forms such as 'gentlemen' or the surname on its own, and it may be that the higher status person can also exercise more choice than subordinates in the form used and hence take the initiative in defining the situation. When I was a student on teaching practice I called the register of my new fourth year class using only their surnames, as this is what I had been used to as a pupil. All seemed to go smoothly until I checked whether one girl who had not answered was absent. The class assured me that she was, in fact, present and pointed her out to me. When I asked why she had not answered her name she replied 'I've got a handle to my name' which, in my innocence, I had to get translated. I had unwittingly expressed my relationship to her in a way which did not coincide with her understanding, and as I was only a student she felt able to tell me. Had I been the headteacher she might have accepted this definition or at least felt more inhibited about challenging it.

One may, of course, address pupils without speaking as when giving a non-verbal direction such as beckoning (see Figure 21). This is certainly an expression of higher status, as pupils do not give such directions to teachers. In a similar way, it is not unusual to see a teacher pointing at a pupil. Gesturing towards the addressee is usually associated with giving particular emphasis or instructing them and is therefore an appropriate part of the teacher's non-verbal repertoire. Pupils are less likely to gesture towards teachers, perhaps because they are not often in the position of being able to tell them anything they don't already know, and

Figure 21 *An unspoken command.*

it is therefore very unusual to see them pointing at teachers (Galloway, 1979). In Figure 22 the girl is feeling very indignant about being questioned by the headteacher about the suitability of her clothes as she believes he has previously accepted them. The fact that she is waving her finger at him not only expresses this indignation but also the informal relationship which exists between them. With a more 'distant' authority figure, she would feel less able to point. Pointing with the palm up gives an impression of offering a view in a reasonable way, whereas, at the other extreme, a stabbing, palm down movement, together with the head

Figure 22   *'But you said I could wear them!'*

thrust forward is clearly aggressive and an attempt to dominate the interaction. Most teachers would feel very uncomfortable if pupils felt able to behave in such ways towards them.

Forms of address, then, are not fixed. The changes which occur may reflect temporary circumstances, attempts to convey particular impressions, or developments in the relationships between people. Where there are status differences, these are reflected in the differences in rights to use a familiar or sometimes other chosen form. There are, no doubt, many other subtle ways in which status differences are expressed. In particular it is likely that the tone of voice and other vocal aspects such as hesitations, convey one's understanding of the status relationship. However, apart from the difficulty of describing vocal changes adequately in the written medium, they are more concerned with one's manner, giving the listener impressions about the speaker's confidence or emotional state.

In the light of the examples discussed so far, it is possible to gather together the points made to consider what the nature of authority relationships might be.

2 The Nature of Authority

In considering the nature of authority, the concept of 'the definition of the situation' (Thomas, 1931) is particularly relevant, as it is concerned with the understandings people hold in any interaction and the expectations they have, based on these understandings. Some situations are already well 'defined', as in a court of law, but in classrooms there is a good deal of scope for individual interpretations as is evident from the wide range of practices and conduct which can be observed. In such situations Goffman (1959) suggested that people usually try to influence the type of understandings which will prevail:

> Regardless of the particular objective which the individual has in mind and of his motive for having this objective, it will be in his interests to control the conduct of others, especially their responsive treatment of him. This control is achieved by influencing the definition of the situation which the others come to formulate, and he can influence this definition by expressing himself in such a way as to give them the kind of impression that will lead them to act voluntarily in accordance with his own plan.

When pupils behave as subordinates, they presumably act in accordance with the teacher's definition of the situation, which is one in which he is permitted to exercise control. What influences pupils to accept the teacher's authority may vary in different situations, as will the extent of that authority, and some of the factors will be discussed later in this chapter. However, the definition which is formed is concerned with the nature of the relationship between the teacher and pupils and, in particular, the status difference between them. Once there is an agreement between the participants about the nature of their relationship, this will influence the details of their interactions but the converse is also true: in situations which are initially 'loosely' defined, the details of the interaction will influence the form of agreement reached.

Relationships are not simply beliefs that people have about the way they should interact with other people, they are expressed and negotiated in the actions themselves and in the manner in which those actions are performed. Relationships exist *through* our interactions, where our total behaviour, both verbal and non-verbal, can be seen from two points of view. First, it is to some extent determined by the understanding which the participants already have of the existing relationship and in this sense it is an expression of that understanding. Second, it can be seen as an attempt by the participants either to restate or to modify that understanding. This view is quite consistent with that proposed by Stubbs (1976) and Torode (1976) who placed an emphasis on verbal communication in this process, but there has also been an attempt here to highlight the significant aspects of non-verbal behaviour which express and influence the status relationship as the interaction proceeds. When the teacher chose to address one child as 'darling' and another as 'young lady' (p.36), she was, at a surface level, simply comforting one and admonishing the other. At a deeper level, she was exercising a right to behave in such ways towards those pupils. In exercising unilateral rights, such as using the other's personal space and property, or touching them, the teacher makes a claim to have the degree of authority implied. There is no guarantee that pupils will accept such treatment and it is only in their reactions that the relationship is continually validated or redefined. When I first began teaching I was supervising the fifth year boys who were changing after a games period. They were taking a long time and I could hear them discussing the game they had just played, so I put my head round the door of the changing room and made what would now be considered a sexist gibe: 'Come along *girls*, stop the nattering and get changed.' The reply from one boy was immediate: 'All right Miss, we won't be long.' The original presentation of the relationship I had claimed had not been accepted, at least by one of the pupils, and he had expressed his understanding by claiming similar rights. He was prepared to grant me some authority but not the extent that I had implied. Some pupils are far less skilful in their attempts to modify their relationships with teachers, and bitter confrontations can follow.

On the pupils' part, for example, when they warily enter teachers' territories, assume upright postures and face teachers, they are presenting themselves as subordinates and thereby *investing* authority in the teacher. Of course, such behaviours might be thought of simply as polite, which they are, but we convey subordination in additional ways such as in our bodily tension, facial expression and tone of voice. 'Politeness' may be according 'mock' respect without these additional cues but what would clearly claim a status difference in the relationship would be the failure of the other to return such courtesies by remaining relaxed in posture, not facing and using the territory freely. By the processes of claims which are legitimised or challenged by pupils, and investments which are accepted or refused by teachers, relationships are continually restated or modified.

There are obviously degrees of authority in a relationship; at one extreme where, say, a religious leader is treated with reverence in any context by his followers and at the other extreme, anyone with relevant specialised knowledge in an emergency who would be granted limited authority, as long as the emergency lasted. Teachers are often accorded a degree of authority in out-of-school contexts by their pupils, beyond that which would be given to other familiar adults. It is interesting to speculate whether the extent of the authority which exists in a relationship might be observed from the range of different contexts in which the differential rights occur and also in the extent of those rights. Subordinate behaviours may also be highly exaggerated, such as in the 'attention' posture in the Armed Services, and it may be that the degree of status difference is also detectable in the extent of the exaggeration. Mehrabian's dimension of relaxation-tension seems particularly relevant here in assessing the degree of subordination in the behaviour.

The question of whether subordinate behaviour is voluntary or involuntary is an important consideration which reflects upon the distinction between authority and power. Do pupils behave as subordinates because they respect teachers or because they fear them? In a discussion of Weber's (1958) analysis of power, persuasion and authority, Spady (1973) considered their relevance for teachers. Power is the probability of carrying out one's will in a social situation, despite resistance from others. One can observe the same behaviours in power relationships as those that occur in status relationships, as described earlier in this chapter but the important difference is that the subordinate is *compelled* to act in such ways and accept such treatment. A teacher's power, then, is the capacity to make pupils do what they do not wish to do, and many would argue that this capacity is becoming increasingly limited. Even when pupils do comply unwillingly to avoid unpleasant consequences the situation is far from satisfactory as Spady points out:

> Given that such compliance is essentially involuntary, the resulting condition is usually an uneasy, short-term truce the subordinate party accepts with resentment and hostility, making stable and cooperative social arrangements between parties highly unlikely.

The power to coerce or reward to ensure compliance, and the associated dangers, should not be confused with the exercise of institutional power within an authority agreement. If one compares an army camp with a wartime concentration camp there will be many similarities in the behaviour of subordinate with superior ranks, to that of the prisoners with guards. The guards only needed to use dominant behaviour when the prisoners failed to comply and the same would be true of the army camp. The essential difference is that in the army the power of the superiors is accepted as part of the relationship, whereas in the concentration camp, compliance was forced *because of the power*, which was very much in evidence in the barbed wire and firearms. Once this power had gone there was no compliance whereas in the army, authority relationships are frequently sustained in circumstances where the superior no longer has any real power over the subordinate. In an authority agreement, therefore, the superior may also have a range of powers over the subordinate and the right to use them fairly would be accepted. However, the relationship is not maintained by those powers but by the respect granted by the subordinates and earned by the superiors.

In some schools there may be very formal relationships where expressions of power, such as the right to use imperatives in control instructions (see p.55) are accepted by the pupils. In others, teachers will go to great lengths to avoid expressions of status difference. In either case the particular relationships must be understood, agreed and maintained on the basis of effective and sympathetic teaching as it is not sensible or feasible to attempt to maintain them by the use of powers to punish or reward.

It is possible for either the teacher or the pupil to define an interaction as one where force will determine the outcome, rather than cooperation. The teacher who intervenes with an unambiguous expression of power, implying 'Do it, or else' thereby denies the pupil any opportunity to present his compliance as a voluntary act. For example, the long and insulting harangue delivered by Mr Baker in response to a pupil apparently chewing (p.115) immediately defines any compliance as capitulation. ('I can enforce it and I will.') On the other hand, the following example of the build-up of a confrontation, reported by the teacher, shows the pupil forcing the issue of power:

> I noticed that he was sitting next to Tony again. Last week I'd separated them – they seemed to distract each other so much. I decided I couldn't let it pass, but neither did I particularly want to make an issue of it. So, as I handed out some worksheets, I quietly reminded him that he wasn't to sit next to Tony until further notice. Would he please move? A few stragglers came in and I'd to sort out a few kids who'd forgotten their exercise books. I kept thinking 'why on earth doesn't he just move – quietly and without a fuss'. I didn't want an incident. By now the class was settled and expectant. He was still sitting, head down, next to Tony. I'd have to try again.
>
> 'Move over here, please,' I said, pointing to an empty desk at the far side of the class.
>
> 'Why should I? Why don't you move him instead of me?'
>
> 'I'm not asking him. I'm *telling* you,' I said with as much authority as I could muster. 'Move now!'
>
> The class had gone very quiet. Some eyes were on him. Most were fixed on me. There was a gathering sense of excitement.
>
> 'Make me,' he said.

If the teacher is giving an accurate description of his behaviour, the first two instructions were tactful (see p.97) but the pupil chose not to comply voluntarily. The third attempt carried strong overtones of force, so that had the pupil then moved it could only have been construed as a result of the teacher's power rather than the authority agreement. In this case the teacher clearly felt obliged to threaten force in response to the pupil's lack of cooperation.

Once dominant behaviour (as opposed to relaxed, high status behaviour) is used by the teacher it is difficult for the pupil not to either dispute or validate the claim to power. Similarly, if the pupil rejects the authority agreement it is difficult for the teacher not to concede or resort to power. One alternative for both, is to try persuasion and in the previous example the pupil's suggestion that someone else should move might have been a very crude attempt. Persuasion or reasoning with pupils may eventually ensure voluntary compliance though this is by no means assured (see p.136). In accepting the necessity for, or the desirability of, persuasion the teacher greatly reduces the status difference presented between himself and the pupils. At an extreme, if pupils exercise the same rights in relation to teachers as teachers do towards them, then, in effect, authority does not exist in the relationship. Some teachers would consider this desirable and there is much to be said for pupils being able to share in the decision-making processes in the school, particularly as they get older. However, there are dangers in relying on persuasion as the teacher may be forced to negotiate and justify every activity which takes place and this can be very time consuming. There is clearly an essential place for reasoning and discussion in schools but the terms under which it is conducted must be carefully established. If a teacher relinquishes power for persuasion, it is easy for a few irresponsible pupils to take control.

The essential feature of an authority relationship is that the subordinate acts voluntarily with the superior's wishes because it is an agreement between them and not because he fears the consequences of disobedience or is persuaded on each occasion that it is in his interests to do so. Authority relationships do not have the dangers of generating hostility in pupils as in power relationships, or of frequent time-consuming negotiations at the pupils' behest if one relies on persuasion. What, then, is the basis for authority? What can induce pupils to grant authority to teachers or, putting it another way, what must teachers do to earn respect from pupils?

All teachers have the same institutional authority and the same legal powers in relation to pupils. For the most part, they can all call on the same sanctions, though the higher status teachers usually control the administration of the more serious sanctions such as suspension from school. The considerable differences in authority granted to teachers in the same school, regardless of age, sex and seniority, must therefore be derived from the different personal qualities they demonstrate, rather than from the positions they hold. As Tattum (1982) pointed out:

> Respect for the teacher *qua* teacher can no longer be assumed as a social fact. No longer is the office held in awe and teachers who draw heavily upon unquestioned authority as an endowed right leave themselves open to mimicry and ridicule.

Tattum and Spady express the view shared here, that the basis for this personal authority rests largely on the effectiveness of one's teaching and all that this entails, together with the concern shown for one's pupils, in particular for their educational welfare. In short, if one does not teach effectively, if one is boring, unprepared and disinterested in the pupils' efforts, one cannot expect to be granted authority. However, it would be naive to believe that effective teaching alone will always result in respect from pupils, and subsequent chapters will not only explore aspects of effective teaching such as self-presentation and group management, but will also consider those occasions when pupils still fail to accept the teacher's authority in the relationship.

The nature of the teacher-pupil relationship changes not only as particular relationships develop, but also as pupils mature and grow in independence throughout their schooldays. Tanner (1978) suggested that discipline in schools has an educative function as well as simply to provide a context in which teaching can take place. She argued that educative discipline is necessary if children are to develop through 'disciplinary stages' that run parallel to the cognitive stages of development suggested by Piaget. Children move from a largely dependent and responsive stage where the teacher is responsible for their behaviour, to the stage where they are self-directed and expected to exercise leadership where appropriate. Teachers may facilitate this process by exercising the form of discipline which encourages the child to move to the next stage of development. Another way of viewing the process that Tanner describes and avoiding the controversy that surrounds the notion of 'stages', is that if pupils are to learn to act responsibly, teachers must gradually give up their authority and essentially grant it to pupils in some circumstances.

Just as pupils mature and develop, so teachers become older and more experienced. This too has implications for the form of relationship which they can expect with their pupils. Because of these various factors concerning the pupils, teachers and the contexts in which they meet, it is very dangerous to be prescriptive about how teachers should or should not behave, and the reader will no doubt be able to find circumstances where any advice or view expressed here does not seem appropriate. What a teacher chooses to do not only depends on what he wishes to achieve, but also on what he believes the children will allow him to do. It is probable that one reason why student and probationary teachers frequently have problems of discipline is because they themselves are not clear about the form of relationship, and all that this entails, which they wish to have with their pupils (Wragg and Wood, 1984a). If they are not absolutely clear in their own minds how much authority they can expect to have and what is, therefore, acceptable or not acceptable behaviour, they cannot possibly make this clear to their pupils. The process of establishing and maintaining the authority relationship one deems appropriate involves confidently expressing that relationship in one's behaviour, teaching effectively so that one's claims are seen as legitimate, and also dealing effectively with those who still attempt to challenge that relationship. In this latter respect, any pupil who persists in disrupting a well-prepared and appropriately pitched lesson, and who does not respond to requests from the teacher to comply, can be thought of as unreasonably challenging the authority relationship by his actions. It will then be necessary for the teacher to use persuasion or even to resort to power to assert the status difference in the relationship. On the other hand, boring and disinterested teachers must expect to be continually challenged as they have not established the major basis for the authority they claim.

In the illustration shown earlier (Figure 1, p.3) the pupil has been asked to remain behind because of persistent talking during the lesson. The relaxed posture, leaning against the wall with hands in pockets, clearly expresses his resentment and will be perceived by most teachers as disrespectful. The pupil is refusing to adopt a polite, if not subordinate, attentive posture which would be appropriate in such formal circumstances but there are no hard and fast rules which can govern the teacher's response. How one reacts will be influenced by what treatment one feels the pupil needs and will also accept. Is it really necessary to make the pupil stand up straight so that he accepts his subordinate position? This might be achieved by giving a sharp command which is clearly a display of dominance aimed at asserting the power difference. Even if this were thought desirable, such action might well be resisted by the pupil and the teacher would have little option but to escalate the confrontation further. Before considering such an approach one must be certain that the pupil will comply. In contrast, one could ignore the obvious disrespect and continue to deal with the problem in a relaxed, non-threatening manner. This does not treat the pupil's behaviour as a serious challenge as the teacher maintains high status behaviour, and it is possible that the pupil might automatically change his posture as he begins to feel less threatened. However, any sign of uncertainty on the teacher's part might convey to the pupil that he is weak and has backed down from the challenge. To be convincing, the teacher would probably need to feel some genuine sympathy and understanding for the pupil and not wish to humble or intimidate him. It seems sensible, therefore, to interpret the disrespectful display not simply as the result of being publicly held to account, but as a sign that he feels he is being treated unfairly.

If one is in a position *incidentally* to direct a pupil away from the wall physically or lift his hands from his pockets, in a relaxed and unconcerned manner, this will express higher status but also 'remind' the pupil of his responsibility as a subordinate to be attentive. Again, the pupil could resist or otherwise attempt to regain the initiative but the teacher should not then resort to dominance but rather question the pupil's right to resist or ask the reason for his resistance (see p.25).

On another occasion, a pupil might perch on the edge of the teacher's desk while listening to an explanation. Should the teacher 'correct' the action and, if so, how, or should it be taken as a positive sign of a developing relationship? These are questions which only the teacher can answer as one needs to take account of factors such as the context, the existing relationship, how the teacher construes the action and how he wishes the relationship to develop.

It is evident, then, that there can be no foolproof recipe to offer the teacher in such complex circumstances, but those who are uncertain about the nature of their relationships with pupils will be particularly vulnerable. However, in a later chapter p. 138) some general principles relating to confrontations will be discussed and these may be helpful in guiding one's actions.

3 Establishing Authority in First Meetings

It is necessary for the teacher to create a context in which communication can take place, though pupils must increasingly share in this responsibility as they get older. In this discussion of how the authority relationship is established it must be remembered that it is up to each teacher to decide on the extent of authority they feel is appropriate and desirable. This may mean deliberately avoiding or abandoning practices which express status differences in some cases. However, in order to give up one's authority it may first be necessary to establish that one has it and it could be in the teacher's interest to consider the following aspects of teacher-pupil interaction which bear upon the developing relationship.

The significance of first meetings with pupils has already been mentioned and Hargreaves (1972) in his earlier writing reflected the views of many teachers when he described them as battles which the teacher must win.

> Whatever the causes, the phenomenon itself remains. If the teacher does not establish his own dominance, the children are likely to turn the classroom into a circus without a ringmaster and the teacher will become rapidly exhausted and demoralised.

Ball (1980) gives several examples of what some students and teachers described as the 'honeymoon' of the first lesson, when pupils are passive and essentially 'weighing-up' the teacher. The second stage was, as one pupil described it, when 'the boys muck about to see if they can get away with being stupid'. Ball suggested that this 'information gathering' and 'testing out' may be considered conceptually as having two major purposes. The pupils first find it necessary 'to discover what parameters of control the teacher is seeking to establish over their behaviour' and, second, 'to explore in practice whether or not the teacher has the tactical and managerial skills to defend the parameters he or she is seeking to establish'. This analysis, however, does not bring into consideration the teaching skills which essentially form the basis for any claims the teacher makes to establish certain 'parameters of control' over their behaviour. Pupils will also be influenced by how confident the teacher appears, how interesting they find the lesson and what work demands are made on them, as well as the teacher's ability to enforce any rules of conduct imposed. This process will be further discussed in the next section but the importance of first meetings for subsequent relationships is clear, a point made forcibly by Wadd (1973):

> In establishing the order he has decided upon, the teacher must be fully aware that what happens in the first few encounters with the pupils is likely to establish the relationships which he will have to live with for the rest of his contact with that particular class.

If future negotiations are to take place, as they inevitably will because relationships do not remain static, then it is in the teacher's interests to start from a position of subsequently being able to make concessions to the pupils than vice versa. Wragg and Wood (1984a) found that, at the start of the school year, experienced teachers made a 'massive combined effort ... to establish a working climate for the whole year'. Most of them 'sought to establish some kind of dominant presence ... to temper any initial harshness with humour and convey to their class that they were firmly in charge, using their eyes, movement and gesture to enhance what they were trying to do'. They seemed clear in their minds before the year began how they would conduct themselves, in contrast to the student teachers who were less certain about their rules and aspirations before their teaching practice.

Student teachers rarely have the opportunity of observing an experienced teacher meeting a class for the first time, yet the initial contact may be crucial in determining the later relationships with the pupils. By the time the student observes a class the pattern of the interaction has been established, and the teacher is either comfortably sustaining a satisfactory situation or desperately trying to retrieve an unsatisfactory one. Quite understandably a headteacher does not usually allow students to observe the latter, because of sympathy for the teacher or perhaps guilt that such a state of affairs should exist in his school. This is unfortunate, as there is much to be learned from those who are doing the wrong things, as well as from those who are apparently successful. The temptation for students is to model their own behaviour on the first warm and responsive person they observe or on a teacher they remember from their own schooldays. This can be a big mistake as it is very unlikely that the successful, friendly relationships which are established later bear much resemblance to the relationships in the first meetings.

If pupils learn that they need not attend to the teacher and can, to a large extent, control his behaviour, some of them will not surrender this power easily and it only takes a few to disrupt a lesson. Once any relationship is established it is difficult for one partner to alter it in ways which the other considers disadvantageous and persuasion may not be sufficient. A teacher who has established a controlled but not repressive working atmosphere will find that pupils will tolerate the occasional lapse in the standard of teaching whereas a class which has developed into 'a circus without a ringmaster' may still not attend even when the lesson is well planned, interesting and relevant.

Whenever pupils are asked what characteristics they value in teachers they invariably include the ability to keep control in the class (for example, White and Brocking, 1983; Wragg and Wood, 1984a). In practice it might seem that they do all they can to prevent this happening but the paradox could be explained by the fact that usually only a small proportion of pupils are persistently disruptive. A teacher who sets out to gain control will probably have the support of the majority of pupils, provided that he is also seen as fair and not 'boring'. Those who are authoritarian and confrontational will be disliked and resented as Wragg and Wood concluded after observing a teacher who was universally disliked by his pupils:

> Those who wish to make a firm start and establish control should recognise that, whilst pupils can see the need for and even expect such a beginning, if they are over-bossy or fail to temper their authority with humanity, they may never secure a positive working relationship with their class.

Confidence and firmness

Imagine a situation where you are driving towards a junction and the traffic lights begin to change as you approach. You decide it is too late to stop and manage to cross without any problems arising. Very shortly afterwards a car overtakes you and the driver indicates that you should stop. You do so, pulling up behind his car. He gets out and walks unhurriedly towards you, looking at your number plate as he approaches. Reaching your window, he looks down at you and says 'Good afternoon, Sir. Are you the owner of this vehicle?' Most students and teachers agree that their first assumption would be that the driver had some authority to stop you, probably because he was an off-duty policeman. The measured, confident approach, the characteristic language and your own expectations, having just committed a minor traffic offence, would all influence this assumption. What is less obvious, but probably more important, is that only the Police would be expected to stop a member of the public in such circumstances. Anyone carrying out such an action is therefore likely to be taken for a policeman. In a similar way, any adult in a school who exercises rights towards pupils which normally only teachers exercise, is likely, initially, to be taken for a teacher. However, just as one would want to see some identification from the driver to prove that he had the authority he was claiming, so pupils would have to be convinced that the adult's claim to have authority was legitimate. As suggested earlier, this would rest more on the capacity of the adult being able to demonstrate that he could teach effectively, than simply on having the institutional status of teacher, though this would initially be an advantage. Ideally one's teaching should always be stimulating, pitched at the right level for each individual and carried out with warmth and concern for the pupils. Unfortunately, it is not always possible to achieve this standard but it is never more important to try than in one's first meetings with pupils as this is the essential basis for one's claim to be granted authority.

In the example above, the confident, unhurried manner in which the driver approached and his use of characteristic language also contributed to the perceived legitimacy of the action. They gave the impression of his being experienced in such matters and of being secure in the right to take such actions. If the posture had been tense and the vocal and facial expressions had shown doubt or anxiety then you would immediately begin to question the authority claimed in stopping you and asking questions. The nature of our claim is expressed in the actions we carry out but our security in making that claim, our belief that we have a legitimate right to behave as we do, is expressed in the *manner* in which the actions are performed. One factor, therefore, which influences whether pupils accept a teacher's treatment of them is the degree of confidence with which the teacher behaves. Experienced teachers often advise students to behave confidently when facing a class as this helps in establishing good classroom control. If we feel confident or self-assured there is an implication that we expect others to respond appropriately and that even if they did not, we would be able to manage the situation without difficulty. If we lack confidence, it implies that we feel uncertain about our ability to gain pupils' attention and deal effectively with any problems. Like all good self-fulfilling prophesies this is usually just what happens. If the teacher feels confident, the pupils are noticeably more responsive and this in turn reinforces his own assurance; if the teacher lacks confidence, the process can begin in reverse, and he can quickly become thoroughly demoralised.

It follows then that such feelings must have very obvious effects on our behaviour as it is through behaviour that feelings are communicated. Mehrabian's relaxation-tension dimension again seems very relevant in this respect, as relaxed behaviour is consistent with high status and also implies that one does not feel threatened. It is easy to say that one should appear relaxed but it is very difficult to control feelings of anxiety and these can usually be detected from the tone of voice and other non-verbal behaviour. Only the brilliant actors will be able to hide such signs and the best that most of us can do is to reduce any possible reasons for feeling anxious by being thoroughly prepared and regarding the pupils as friendly rather than hostile. The discussion in the next chapter on non-verbal communication of feelings may also be helpful.

It is also sometimes recommended that a new teacher should be firm at first and ease off later as it is much more difficult to be firm after one has been lax at the outset. This traditional advice may be quite sound but unfortunately fails to describe what being 'firm' entails. Some interpret firmness as coming down like a hammer on the first child who does the slightest thing wrong, but then often find themselves in a confrontation with a pupil. Kounin (1970) attempted to identify features of firmness, so that observers could rate teachers for this behaviour. He suggested that it meant the degree to which the teacher conveyed 'I – mean – it' and 'now!' in a *desist* order. This is open to question as there seems to be a strong suggestion of threat in Kounin's description, which implies that the pupil might choose not to follow the instruction. The threat is a warning not to make such a choice. Kounin goes on to say that the message of an instruction should have *clarity* – it should stand out from whatever the teacher was previously doing, and provide a sharp contrast. High message clarity would be conveyed by the teacher making a clean break from a previous location in the room, stopping his previous activity, giving a warning signal and using a tone of voice that stands out. The other aspect of firmness Kounin mentions is the *follow through*, which entails moving closer to the deviant, looking firmly at him during and for a while after the instruction, using a *physical assist* (e.g. leading by the arm), and using a *repeat urge*. That is *not* a repeat in response to failure.

This description clearly shows aspects of aggressive threat on the teacher's part, which is again a debatable aspect of firmness. Also, the 'physical assist' would surely be an unwise act, unless the teacher is a great deal stronger than the child and is sure of no resistance. 'Mr Howie' (in Torode, 1976) found this out to his cost:

> John Cannon was slow in entering the class one day, when Mr Howie was directly behind him. The teacher said, 'Get in, Cannon', and pushed him. Cannon held his ground and engaged in struggle. He laughed, and appeared to find it a great joke, for he said 'What a weakling!' as the teacher had to concede defeat.

As discussed earlier, physical direction, as an alternative to a verbal instruction, can be very effective but should never involve force, nor should it be accompanied by the other non-verbal threats described as aspects of 'follow through'. A pupil who is talking as he enters the room with his classmates might be quietly guided to one side, or a teacher might remove a pen from the hand of a pupil who is writing at the wrong moment, without the teacher interrupting what he is saying to the rest of the class. It is surely the teacher's ability to do this, or to give a verbal instruction, in such a way that the thought of resistance does not enter the pupil's head, which is an essential quality of firmness. To be firm one must be confident and this can only arise from a belief or certainty in one's legitimate right to behave as one does. If we consider the example of taking a pupil aside because he is talking as he enters the room, the manner in which this act is performed is likely to reflect the strength of the teacher's belief that the pupil should not be talking at that time, and that he has the right to stop him. Firmness should have no overtones of force as this can provoke a confrontation and it is noticeable that experienced teachers frequently carry out such actions incidentally, while apparently attending to other matters. This is particularly so when the intervention involves a physical direction (see p.25) and looking away may serve to mitigate any aggressive connotations. Confidence and firmness, then, arise from being certain in one's own mind that the actions one is taking are necessary and that one has a legitimate right to take them.

In their interactions with pupils, teachers present claims to particular relationships (in actions), express degrees of confidence in those claims (in manner) and present 'credentials' (in teaching skills) on which the claims are based. The pupils, for their part, may be doing similar things and hence the definition of the situation is negotiated. This process goes on all the time but is particularly relevant during first meetings.

Addressing the class

When I lecture to a group of postgraduate students who have recently arrived at college or experienced teachers on courses, I am sometimes able to start by giving a clear instruction after clapping my hands sharply, 'Right, stop the noise and pay attention.' The teachers usually laugh because they know I have to be joking no matter how convincing I have tried to appear. The students usually stop talking but look at me in disbelief as being new to the college they are far less certain of their own status. Although the instruction is quite functional, using the imperative form claims a degree of power which few people would accept. For adults to comply unquestioningly with such commands they would have to be subordinates in organisations such as the Armed Forces or inmates of a prison, where their superiors would also have considerable powers over them. In a Court of Law the injunction 'Silence in Court' is not questioned and it would express a very different relationship if the usher asked, 'Do you think we could have a little quiet please?' Such a form is more appropriate when giving a lecture as it conveys a more equal relationship with the audience. The lecturer cannot claim the same power as a court usher or even a teacher, and the authority granted is largely on the basis of the students requiring the knowledge one is communicating. Teachers often use the more 'polite' forms not necessarily because they do not have the power implied by the use of commands but because they wish to characterise the relationship as cooperative (see p.111).

Teachers frequently need to gain silence and attention from pupils and it is evident that the particular contact signals they use express their understanding of the situation and of the relationships. The functional attribute of contact signals is that they should be loud enough to be heard or noticeably visible. In a room where pupils are working silently it would be sufficient to say quietly 'Could you just stop what you're doing and pay attention please?', but if there is any noise in the room a louder intervention would be called for.

It is desirable to have silence and attention when anyone, teacher or pupil, is addressing the class but as this entails everyone stopping whatever is being done, the message must be important enough to warrant the interruption. If pupils are busily working, frequent intervention will only upset their concentration. It might be possible to leave the message until later, or perhaps it concerns only a few pupils who could be approached individually.

A common habit with some teachers is to shout out a request for the class to stop talking or pay attention, and then quickly continue with the message in a raised voice before the noise has subsided. The expectation is that the pupils will hear the teacher talking and attend, but this can take a considerable time during which some of the message may be missed. The children are also learning that they need not respond to requests for silence, and on future occasions the talking may persist for increasing periods of time. The teacher, in turn, has to raise his voice in an attempt almost to smother their talking with his own noise, so that they are unable to communicate with each other. *'I'm not going to tell you again* 2W. *Stop all talking and pay attention to me. Alan Baker! Did you hear what I said?'* This generally briefly interrupts most other communication in the room and the noise lessens but, surprisingly, many teachers will often begin to talk again before there is complete silence, and the noise slowly builds up once more. From the outset it should be established that the class has to attend when told to as it is important not to teach them to ignore one's signals.

As suggested, the form of contact one chooses can express a definition of the situation and it may therefore vary from occasions where it prefaces information about a task, to interventions where it presages a reprimand. An unconventional example is quoted by Stubbs (1976):

> At the start of one English class which I observed, the teacher, after talking quietly to some pupils at the front of the room, turned and said to the whole class: 'Right! Fags out, please!' No pupils were smoking so the teacher did not mean his words to be taken literally. I interpret his remark as having a primary function of attracting the pupils' attention, of warning them of messages still to come – in short, of opening the communication channels. The remark had a 'contact' function of putting the teacher *in touch* with the pupils.

The humorous and esoteric nature of this message expresses a close and informal relationship and it would be unlikely if the teacher had then followed with any serious critical remarks. Humorous instructions are probably not appropriate when first meeting a class because the relationship between the teacher and pupils has not developed sufficiently to allow them, and they might be seen as attempts to ingratiate oneself.

The form of speech used, the humour, and the non-verbal behaviour all not only contribute to and develop a relationship, but must be expressions of that relationship so far. This interdependence of communication and context is pointed out by Stubbs:

> Speech is therefore not just something that happens *in* situations – a sort of epiphenomenon. It is part *of* situations. To say, therefore, ... that certain situations 'determine' certain kinds of language-use is to over simplify. It is, rather, a two way process ... the characteristic 'contact' language of teachers creates, and is created by, a specific social situation in the classroom.

In the same way, when Mrs Newman asked Carol where she had been and was told 'Shut your mouth' (Furlong, 1976), or when Alan Jones was told to leave the room by Mr Howie and replied 'Get stuffed' (Torode, 1976), these pupils' language not only affects subsequent events but is an expression of the type of relationship which exists between the teacher and pupils. It is characteristic of the control exercised by the pupils that, in both these instances, they do not respond appropriately to the teachers but 'turn the tables' so that the teacher must react in some way. In so doing they are challenging the teacher's definition of the status relationship, and expressing their own. Such situations rarely develop immediately. They are usually the product of previous meetings during which the pupils have gained in confidence and learned that they can speak to those teachers in that way.

With a new group the form of teacher-pupil relationship has yet to be established. It has not been determined whether there will be a friendly cooperative atmosphere, or one in which pupils are either repressed or can tell the teacher to 'get stuffed'. Informal language from either side could be premature, and the teacher would risk sacrificing some authority. It would therefore be safer to rely on conventional ways of gaining attention, such as banging a board rubber, clapping, or saying in a raised voice, 'Pay attention everyone' but, whatever one does it must be clearly established that when attention is called for it is an instruction and not a request. Absolute silence must be achieved before the message is given. The class must learn at the outset to be quiet when anyone, including one of their own members, is addressing them.

It is often preferable at the start of a lesson to establish contact without having to say anything, as at this time one should *expect* attention from the pupils. The novelty of a new teacher entering the room will usually gain attention and silence, particularly if he stands confidently and prominently in front of the group. As a general rule, the less one has to say to gain attention, the better. If it were possible to quell a rowdy mob simply by entering the room this would, by inference, reflect the considerable authority or power of the person entering. It follows that if one has to go to great lengths to get attention from a group who are simply talking, one lacks authority in the relationship. If the teacher considers that the class is not paying sufficient heed, then the form of instruction chosen is important as it expresses one's definition of the situation.

When complete silence is achieved it is possible to talk in a normal voice, or even a little quieter than usual, which emphasises the pupils' responsibility to listen. If one wishes to make any point forcibly then either lowering or raising one's voice, when there is absolute silence and attention, will have a dramatic effect provided it is not done too frequently. It is never advisable to compete with noise in a room by shouting above it, other than to give a signal for attention. This can become a habit, so that teachers always talk loudly over the noise in the room, and this gives the voice a boring quality, as the vocal variations are reduced in the effort to make oneself heard.

There is no need to deliver a lengthy lecture on behaviour when pupils have been slow to attend, though some teachers might want to discuss the need for certain rules at this stage. What is essential is for the teacher to establish his requirements by what he does. Having gained silence and begun to talk it is vital to be aware of the first pupil who shows any intention of talking or who is clearly not attending. The teacher need only stop talking in mid-sentence to interrupt him, as the resultant silence will be immediately noticeable. Obviously, this tactic will have little effect if there is so much noise that many pupils are hardly aware that the teacher is talking, and so do not notice if he stops. Pupils can also learn that a particular teacher will not do much if they don't attend or, regrettably, may have little worth attending to. For the best effect, when the teacher breaks off in mid-sentence this should leave near silence in the room. It can therefore only be used to gain attention from a pupil when the great majority of the class is already attending. Then, when a teacher can reliably gain pupils' attention and a personal relationship begins to develop, he can express his own personality, whether it be with a 'Fags out, please' or something a little more formal.

In summary, it has been argued that authority exists in a relationship and is to a large extent granted by the pupils. This implies a cooperative understanding in teacher-pupil relationships. It is in everyone's interest that there should be a context in which teaching and learning can take place and teachers should only have sufficient authority to secure this. For their part, they will have to earn their authority by the quality of their teaching, but it is also helpful from the outset to behave as if they already have it.

When a person behaves in a confident and efficient manner we are inclined to believe that such behaviour reflects knowledge and experience. In the school situation the reality is that teachers *are* in positions of authority in relation to pupils, but their behaviour must be consistent with this and hence imply knowledge and experience; thus the teacher can claim authority in his first meetings with pupils, but it can easily be eroded. First, he may lack the knowledge and expertise he needs. His lessons could be poorly prepared or badly presented so that the pupils become bored. He might fail to deal quickly and effectively with any problems which arise. Second, his characterisation of the situation could be inadequate – his behaviour might be inconsistent with that of a person in authority. He could be too responsive to the pupils or show signs of anxiety or submission. Third, some pupils might openly challenge his definition of the situation as one in which he is in authority, by lack of cooperation or disruptive behaviour. In this event, the teacher might need the support of senior staff or reliable procedures in the school, which would confirm and reinforce his status. If this support does not exist, then the reality of his authority is in question. There is then the possibility of the pupils beginning to impose their own definition of the situation, in spite of the ascribed status of the teacher.

In the first meetings with new classes, the task for the teacher is mainly one of reinforcing his initial authority. If the pupils successfully manage to challenge or disregard that authority, then subsequent meetings will express the pupils' definition of the situation. The teacher will then be faced with attempting to modify or redefine that definition. Though not impossible, this requires much more effort than merely consolidating or reinforcing an initial definition which is in the teacher's favour, and Goffman's words can be seen as having particular relevance for teachers here:

> It would seem that an individual can more easily make a choice as to what line of treatment to demand from and extend to others present at the beginning of an encounter than he can alter the line of treatment that is being pursued once the interaction is under way.

Though it is vital for a teacher to convey from the outset that he is in authority, the basis of his long-term authority rests in his superior knowledge and ability to communicate effectively. Pupils who regard lessons as uninteresting and pointless are more likely to challenge the teacher, and the next chapter will explore the ways in which a speaker can sustain a listener's attention and convey enthusiasm for his subject.

4 Conveying Enthusiasm

Good classroom control does not rest solely on the ability to act as if one is in authority: the teacher must demonstrate at the outset that he is keen to communicate his subject in a committed and organised manner, or it will quickly become evident that his authority has no legitimate basis. It is in such skills as organising, presenting, communicating and monitoring that the teacher's actual authority rests. Without them he will fail to capture the interest of his pupils or to gain their respect, and his attempts to retain control by wielding power will be resented. The skills of communicating effectively are easy to recognise but difficult to describe, and this may be one reason why they have been neglected in comparison with other aspects of successful teaching. It is essential to communicate in a lively and compelling way and in this chapter there will be an attempt to draw attention to the characteristic and subtle ways in which enthusiasm is conveyed.

Sustaining pupils' attention

People watching an interesting television programme are not easily distracted, and they may even be reluctant to switch the set off when an unexpected visitor calls. Teachers rarely exercise such magnetic power over pupils in their classes, who often attend only out of a sense of duty or fear. Any alternative to a teacher who drones on and on is readily sought or created. Though it is not possible for every lesson to be exciting, the moral is clear: children who are interested and involved in the lesson will attend more, misbehave less and consequently be more likely to learn something. Evidence to support this was presented by Rosenshine (1970), who summarised the results of studies into 'enthusiastic teaching' and concluded that if pupils rated teachers as 'stimulating', 'energetic', 'mobile', 'enthusiastic' and 'animated', this was related to increased pupil achievement scores on tests given at the end of the lesson.

Enthusiastic teaching could be regarded as something of a performance by the teacher. Ross (1978) makes just this point in relation to lecturing:

One writes 'performance' because this is what a good lecture often is. The language of the theatre does not come amiss here; the tyro is directed not to turn his or her back on the audience, to articulate clearly, to project, to maintain eye contact, to practise timing, to use gestures appropriately, to relate to his audience, etc., etc.

This does not mean that teachers are always performers and can never relate to children in genuine ways, or that they must never reveal their 'true' personalities and feelings. What it does mean is that certain aspects of teaching call for special skills; skills such as sustaining attention, establishing control, organising and selecting materials and monitoring pupils' work. If teachers are competent in these skills, then this can only enhance their capacity to make genuine relationships with pupils. On the other hand, the incompetent teacher will always be preoccupied with his own survival.

As Rosenshine's survey suggested, enthusiasm is considered important in sustaining a listener's attention by displaying a strong interest in a subject, almost in a persuasive way. Of course, it is possible to show enthusiasm without necessarily capturing other people's interest, and most of us have been bored by a fanatic who insists on going into minute detail about his personal passion. Rosenshine nevertheless demonstrated that successful teachers were judged as being enthusiastic in their performance, so it seems that enthusiastic teaching must involve not only a strong interest in the subject, but also a need and ability to communicate that interest to others. Here the boring fanatic fails: he is insensitive to the feelings of his listeners. Any communicator, be he teacher, salesman, politician or actor, must always be searching for the listeners' reactions and modifying his performance accordingly.

But what constitutes an enthusiastic performance? It seems to be stating the obvious to draw attention to non-verbal behaviours such as movement, gesture, variation in voice and eye contact. In fact, we usually fail to notice such things if they are relevant and appropriate, because they serve to emphasise the meaning of the communication rather than the act. They give the listener additional information, or convey how the speaker feels about the ideas he is expressing. As Argyle (1975) put it, they provide 'the message about the message'. It is only when non-verbal behaviour is inconsistent with the verbal message that we may begin to notice it. If a speaker is fidgeting with a pencil or using exaggerated or repetitive movements, our attention may be drawn to the act of communication and away from the meaning.

Gestures and speech

If we see a group of people talking together, or a discussion between two people on television, it is easy to identify which person is talking even if we can't hear the sound. Most of the listeners will be looking at that person as, even in a conversation between two people, the listener looks much more at the speaker than vice versa (Kendon, 1967). It will be particularly noticeable that the speaker is moving more than the others, and when he stops talking his body becomes still, as he takes on the role of a listener. The other people in the group will move from time to time, sometimes to give a nod of approval, a smile or some other feedback, perhaps to indicate that they intend to speak. In contrast, the speaker will keep up a fairly continuous stream of nods, and perhaps arm and hand movements, and will change his facial expression from time to time. Any doubt about the extent of these movements is easily dispelled by turning off the sound when a speaker is expressing a forceful point of view on the television. The effect can be quite bizarre, as one is suddenly aware of the vast amount of activity taking place. The more the speaker is emotionally involved in communicating his ideas, the broader and more staccato become the movements. Mehrabian (1972) found that speakers who were trying to be persuasive looked more at their listeners, used more gestures and nods, more facial activity and spoke faster and with less hesitation. If we take the extreme case of two people arguing angrily, we see them directing highly animated behaviour at one another.

Clearly such behaviour serves to sustain the listener's attention, but how does it enhance the meaning of the message? If we look again at an enthusiastic speaker this will become evident. It is important not to choose someone who is attempting to give an objective, unbiased presentation, such as a newsreader, as this affects the bodily behaviour. Someone trying to put over a point of view in a discussion would be ideal. Just as a singer's movements reflect the rhythm of the music and the meaning of the lyrics, so an enthusiastic speaker has a similar relationship with his message. Though he has no music, the words he is using provide their own rhythm. This is determined by the stressed syllables. If we take the word 'rhythm' the stress falls on the first syllable *rhy*thm, whereas in the word 'determined' the stress is on the second syllable, de*ter*mined. We can accentuate some of these stressed syllables more than others by vocal changes in volume, timing and pitch, and this affects the meaning of the message as well as producing a different rhythmic pattern. To illustrate this point, compare two ways of saying the same sentence:

'When we speak . . . we can ac*cen*tuate some of the stressed syllables.' If we alter the vocal stress we make a subtle change in the meaning and affect the rhythm:

'When we speak . . . we can accentuate *some* of the stressed syllables.' The first presentation draws our attention to the capacity to accentuate while speaking, whereas the second implies that only some syllables may be accentuated.

The rhythm which exists in speech is, therefore, determined partly by the normal stresses occurring in words but also by the intended meaning of the communication. The phenomenon seldom noticed by the listener is that bodily movements occur in relation to that rhythm, provided the speaker is relaxed and involved in what he is saying. If we now listen to our speaker on television and attend only to the rhythm, and not to what he is actually saying, the impression we have is that the body is dancing to the rhythm of the speech. This synchronisation of bodily movements with speech rhythms has been observed by many researchers. For example, Kendon (1972) in a careful analysis of a speaker's behaviour noted:

> When such a flow chart of the body movement is matched against a chart showing how the flow of speech sounds changes from frame to frame of the film it is found that these 'configurations of change' occur synchronously with the articulation of the sounds. In other words, the body moves synchronously, and synchronously too, with the changes in the geometry of the oral-pharyngeal regions that occur with speech. Thus as the subject speaks so he moves, the whole organism behaving as an integrated whole.

It should not, of course, seem strange that speech and body movements are frequently synchronised. When a dog barks it does not move its head before or after the bark, but *as* it barks and to a much finer degree the same relationship occurs in human beings.

Kendon (1983) suggested that children's capacity to make use of gesture expands in close association with growth in their capacity for spoken language. Gestures are not an unwanted distraction for the listener, as some would have us believe, but an integral part of the communication. They serve to enhance and clarify the message but, unless they are inappropriate, are seldom noticed by the listener. Some students, when giving video-taped talks, decide to sit on their hands to avoid 'waving them about' but as they relax and become involved, it is quite comical to see their trapped arms flapping like a young bird attempting to fly.

This self-synchrony does not occur all the time. If a person is anxious he may remain quite still when talking apart from fidgeting nervously. The stillness is probably due to muscular tension and the fidgeting can be regarded as a lack of synchrony between speech and movement, which is distracting for the listener. The speaker is concerned with his own anxiety rather than what he is saying. It seems reasonable to suppose, therefore, that the extent to which self-synchrony occurs is an indication of the involvement of the speaker with communicating his ideas. It is also claimed that one can observe the level of a listener's involvement from the extent that he moves in close harmony with the speaker, a phenomenon described as 'interactional synchrony' (Condon, 1976).

Not all movements are rhythmical or emphatic. Sometimes the gesture gives a visual representation of the idea being communicated, particularly of size, shape and position. One instance of this would occur if we asked someone to describe a spiral staircase, but less dramatic examples regularly accompany speech. Some gestures convey specific meaning and can be used in place of words, such as screwing one's finger into the temple to indicate madness. There are relatively few of these and they are obviously learned, as different cultures use different signs for the same concept, just as each has a different verbal language.

Another instance of the clear relationship between gesture and meaning occurs when the movement precedes the word to which it refers, perhaps to suggest an element of uncertainty or choice in the information being conveyed, so that the word is offered as an approx-imation or as one of several alternatives. The gesture occurring before the word, in a brief pause, takes the emphasis away from it. For example, if in the sentence 'It took me (gesture) an hour to get here' the speaker paused briefly before 'an hour', raised his lower lip, looked away and gave an outward movement of the arm or hand, this would indicate that it took approximately an hour. Had the gesture and vocal emphasis fallen on the word 'hour' and been directed towards the listener, we would assume that the journey took exactly or at least an hour and perhaps that the speaker was not very happy about it: 'It took me an *hour* to get here.'

Facial expressions also enhance meaning by showing how the speaker feels about the message. An enthusiastic speaker will be producing a stream of facial expressions which convey his excitment, disbelief, surprise or amusement about his message. Some expressions are extremely brief, lasting about one fifth of a second, and may highlight a particular word, whereas others last much longer, perhaps accompany-ing the verbal expression of an idea. The overall effect is to provide a running commentary for the listener on how the speaker feels about the ideas expressed. In contrast, a speaker who is not involved in his subject shows little variation in facial expression. The impression conveyed is that the ideas are brought out automatically and are failing even to capture the attention of the speaker. This lack of involvement is also communicated by the voice, which sounds regular and monotonous, making it very difficult for a listener to attend for any length of time.

As Kendon (1972) noted from his analysis, the relationship between verbal and non-verbal behaviours can be so precise that one may conclude that whatever mental processes generate the speech also generate the bodily movements:

> It seems that the speech-accompanying movement is produced along with the speech, as if the speech production process is manifested in two forms of activity simultaneously: in the vocal organs and also in bodily movement, particularly in movements of the hands and arms.

Sometimes a speaker will pause for a second or two and look away from the listener, as if gazing into space. At such times most bodily movements also cease, and the impression is that he is thinking what to say next. Such an instance occurred during a lecture on epilepsy, given by a student:

> The child will simply go vacant for up to, probably about twenty seconds, probably no more than that, and several of these could happen during the

day (speaker paused, looked upward and froze all movements for about 1½ seconds except for blinking twice) . . . There will be no falling down, no convulsions, just simply the eyes just go vacant. The major convulsion is of a much more serious nature.

The streams of both verbal and non-verbal behaviour are interrupted when a speaker is searching for, or organising, the next idea. This lack of movement contrasts strongly with the experience of having the idea but not being able to find the right words to express it. This is described as having the word 'on the tip of the tongue' and during such pauses the speaker might trace out fairly small rapid circles with one hand in an impatient way, as well as showing a rather pained or frustrated facial expression.

Bodily movements, therefore, are generated by involvement with the ideas being communicated and are not consciously 'added on'. In order to convey enthusiasm for a subject we must therefore become involved with the ideas and with the need to tell others about them. It would be fatal to concentrate on the movements we are making, as this would inevitably look like 'ham' acting. If we concentrate on communicating the ideas, the movements will take care of themselves, provided we are relaxed and free to move.

To summarise: gestures, bodily movements and facial expressions may be performing a variety of functions in an enthusiastic communication. They may highlight the rhythm of the speech, add emphasis to particular words and phrases, provide visual information about shape, size and position, and sometimes convey specific meaning in place of words. The degree to which this behaviour is related to the rhythm and meaning of the speech provides the listener with an index of the extent to which the speaker is involved with communicating his ideas.

Vocal behaviour and meaning

One need only consider the numerous ways the word 'yes' can be said to recognise how vocal variations play an essential part in conveying meaning (Brazil, 1976). Without variations in timing, pitch and volume, meaning would not only often be ambiguous, but speech would also seem very dull, as if produced by a computer or a very young child when first reading aloud. The word 'monotonous' itself suggests that speech which does not vary in pitch is boring to listen to. Vocal variations are obviously not introduced at random but play a vital role in clarifying and extending the meaning of a communication, as the following brief extract from the lecture on epilepsy illustrates:

> . . . and the most important thing that you must remember here is never, ever, put anything between the teeth. If you put something between their teeth you can break their jaw, or as a policeman did to a girl in the British Epilepsy Association who had a fit down Tottenham Court Road, he put his whistle between her teeth and broke three front teeth.

Argyle (1975) points out that a slower speed of delivery and pauses of more than one fifth of a second give emphasis, and in the passage above the words 'never, ever' are spoken at the rate of two syllables per second, with a clear pause before and after the word 'ever'. The listener is thereby primed to attend to the important information which follows. In contrast, the phrase 'in the British Epilepsy Association who had a fit down Tottenham Court Road' was spoken at a rate of approximately ten syllables per second. Argyle notes that such a rapid rate is used when conveying less important information, such as one might put in brackets when writing, and this is quite consistent with the nature of the information in the phrase above, which serves only to set the scene for the illustrative anecdote. The phrase is also spoken without much variation in pitch, and the impression given is that the speaker is dealing with an irrelevant detail to which the listener need not give much attention. Variations in volume are also evident in the passage, ranging from the emphatic 'never, ever' to a much quieter delivery for the less relevant details.

Vocal variations, therefore, give the listener extra information beyond that conveyed by the words alone. A rise in pitch at the end of an utterance can change a statement into a question; a whining intonation tells us how hard done by the speaker feels; a softer tone may signal that the speaker is attracted to the listener. Of course, a speaker may also need to produce appropriate gestures and facial expression if he is to sound convincing, although the listener may interpret the meaning of the vocal variations correctly from the voice alone.

Eye contact and speech

Kendon (1967) has demonstrated that in normal conversation a listener looks more at a speaker than vice versa. When a speaker looks away his speech becomes less fluent, and Kendon suggested that this may be because he is concentrating on organising what he is about to say; when he looks at the listener, his speech tends to be more fluent. The listener is expected to look more continuously and provide appropriate feedback. If either participant deviates from this expected behaviour particular impressions are conveyed of submission or, perhaps threat.

When a teacher is addressing a group of pupils it is important that he behaves as if he were speaking to each one, and this is achieved mainly by establishing appropriate eye contact. It may not be possible to remember to look at every pupil in the room, though Marland (1975) suggests that this can be achieved if one imagines the room divided into sectors and attends to a different pupil in each. It is important not to let one's eyes wander from person to person in a way which is unrelated to what one is saying. Worse still is the habit which some teachers acquire of looking at the back wall or out of the window when they speak (although it can sometimes be appropriate to do this as it contributes to an impression of 'thinking aloud'). If one delivers discrete sentences or phrases to individuals in the group, not only does one give the impression of speaking to them personally, but it is also possible to see whether they are understanding or concentrating on what is being said. This feedback from individual pupils will, in turn, affect the manner in which the teacher proceeds, just as in a dialogue each must take account of the reactions of the other. Each pupil should feel an active participant in a communication process, rather than merely a passive listener. It is useful to remember that you don't talk to a space as you do to a face, though presumably television presenters are trained to do just this.

A phenomenon associated with eye contact is that, when a speaker is involved in communicating his ideas, even his eyeblinks are affected. Blinks tend to occur at times when they interfere least with the information being communicated, such as during pauses or between ideas, rather than at random during the speech. The previous extracts quoted from the lecture on epilepsy have demonstrated how the speaker's non-verbal behaviour was involved in the communication, and this extended to her blinking. Each blink is indicated by a vertical line.

> |and the most important thing you must remember here is never, ever, put anything between the teeth. | If you put some | thing between the teeth | you can break their jaw | or as a policeman did to a girl in the British Epilepsy Association who had a fit down Tottenham Court Road | he put his whistle between her teeth and broke th|ree front teeth. . . . | so nev|er put anything between the teeth. The other reason is that if | you don't break their jaw | you might, you just might kill them | because there'll be no air coming through | and oxygen to the brain is one of the most important things.

It would also be interesting to measure the speed of the blinks, as they seem to be very rapid during fluent speech, when eye contact is established with the listener, but slower when the speaker has paused briefly.

If a speaker is nervous or for some reason not involved with the ideas he is expressing, blinks may become more frequent and the relationship between speech and blinking no longer takes place. There is evidence to show that blink rate is associated with anxiety (Harris *et al.*, 1966) and increases may be part of the overall difficulty in looking at the listener when one is nervous. The following brief extract taken from a speaker who gave the impression of being rather tense and anxious illustrates this well. The student is describing what she intends to teach to a small group of children on her next school visit:

> Three em | girls who are between nine and te|n and they're above average in mathe|matics a|nd | about average in E|nglish so it was a bit difficult. I don'|t know quite what they're doi|ng in Maths at the moment s|o that I've decided to do | first I'm going to do some|thing on | the topic of fear | because I thought this would be interesting | to them all | and I thought if I went in | to sort | of some of the superstitions an|d about witchcraft and

things like that and then they could, you know, give | a break fo|r the children abou|t um half|way through the morn|ing.

Not only does the speech lack fluency, but the unrelated and frequent blinking increases the disjointed effect of the communication and contributes to the impression of the speaker being nervous.

People vary considerably in the rates at which they blink, but there is a tendency for the pattern of blinking to be affected by their attempt to establish communication with a listener. It is easy to observe this close relationship between speech and blinking in those who are experienced in television appearances or acting. As with other non-verbal behaviours, it is not a conscious process but occurs naturally as the speaker becomes intent on communicating his ideas clearly.

Implications for teaching

This chapter has so far been concerned with the ways in which enthusiasm and other emotions are conveyed. Communicating knowledge and skills is important, but teachers must also display their own enthusiasm if teaching is to be truly effective. It is now possible to consider how certain conditions, familiar to all teachers, affect non-verbal behaviour and hence communication.

Showing inappropriate feelings

Teaching is not simply a process of passing on information to pupils. This could be done in a variety of other ways, but an essential role for the teacher is to create the right attitudes in pupils to gain their interest and involvement. Teaching is an affective process as well as a cognitive one. It is essential therefore that one conveys positive attitudes not only towards one's subject but also towards the pupils.

The quickest way to lose the pupils' attention is to show boredom with the topic being taught. This is a risk that all teachers run, as they are sometimes called upon to repeat the same material to several classes in the course of a year. When one is no longer freshly involved with the ideas being expressed, one's non-verbal behaviour does not enhance the meaning and may even detract from it. It is common to see a speaker fidgeting with an object, and so attention is drawn to that behaviour and away from what is being said. The speaker is, unfortunately, demonstrating that he is insufficiently involved with communicating his ideas, because the bodily movements he makes bear no relation to the rhythm or meaning of his speech. This lack of involvement can also be manifested by a reduction in the variety of non-verbal behaviours so that speech becomes monotonous and the body and face less animated. While the speaker appears otherwise relaxed and fluent, he is perceived as being uninterested in what he is saying, and this feeling is rapidly passed on to the listeners.

The words we choose can also unintentionally reveal unhelpful attitudes. When the teacher begins 'Now, it's a short lesson, so ...' (p.98), this suggests she does not regard it as a proper lesson and what follows confirms this impression. It is never advisable to devalue what one is about to teach and introductions such as 'I had hoped to show you some beautiful slides of the festival but ...', or 'Now I know this is very boring, but we've got to cover this topic', will do little to get the pupils involved. It may be that a teacher has a genuine dislike for the material, and some would argue that it is quite legitimate to express this to the pupils. Surely, though, it is better to present the subject to the best of one's ability and let the pupils decide whether it has any intrinsic merit.

Any circumstances which cause a speaker to be tense or anxious can also create a disjunction between non-verbal behaviour and speech. One's thoughts can be preoccupied by the stressful situation, and consequently the body tends to express this, rather than further the meaning of the speech. Tension also reduces the variation in non-verbal behaviour but, in addition, may produce signs of withdrawal if the speaker is anxious. It is interesting that Mehrabian found that when a speaker was not telling the truth he looked less at the listener, used less gestural and bodily movement, talked less and smiled more. The significance of smiling in stressful situations has already been discussed (see p.32), and these other behaviours would seem to be a product of the anxiety or unease experienced by the speaker.

A nervous speaker may avoid eye contact with his listeners, speak with more hesitation and fidget nervously. This is immediately perceived by the listeners, who may feel uneasy or embarrassed in sympathy. A more common reaction from pupils is to challenge the teacher's authority and thereby increase his anxiety. In order to reduce anxiety it is important to do everything possible to make the lesson run smoothly, particularly with new classes. Insufficient or inadequate preparation can induce stress, and this may distract one's attention from the subject being taught. The teacher may, for example, be worried that there will not be sufficient material for the whole period, or that gaps in his knowledge will be revealed. His body is likely to display this anxiety rather than enhance any ideas he is expressing, and the pupils will soon lose interest. An experienced teacher can cover up or even exploit his lack of knowledge, but it is far easier and safer if one is familiar with the information and has planned its presentation carefully.

The situation itself can be another source of stress. Meeting a new class which has a reputation for being troublesome and unruly can inhibit one's performance. Anxiety should be concealed, and the sooner one can appear relaxed and enthusiastic, the more likely it is that the group will attend. One can promote these conditions by consciously doing a number of things. Positions in the room where one cannot see or be seen by all the pupils should be avoided. Talking to a class while seated at a table or behind a desk inhibits and obscures one's bodily movements, so it is better to stand in such a way that one is free to move. Establishing immediate eye contact with the listeners in a relaxed way also promotes effective interpersonal communication. Avoiding eye contact, adopting tense and static postures, holding on to furniture, fidgeting and other self-effacing behaviours all indicate one's anxiety and detract from any message being conveyed. This makes a difficult situation even worse as some pupils will feel encouraged to challenge one's declining authority. The rest will just be bored.

Figure 23 *'When will you ever learn?'*

It is probably inevitable that teachers will sometimes feel tired and frustrated in their work. Nevertheless, if one reacts with a sudden 'headache' (see Figure 23) when the pupil again fails to get the right answer after a painstaking explanation, or one ushers in the class with a mixture of boredom and resignation, any negative attitudes towards the subject or teacher will be reinforced. Perhaps with the exception of the initial few meetings with a class, a warm and relaxed greeting before the lesson begins will often make all concerned feel better and no matter how many times a lesson has to be repeated, nor how tired one feels, one's involvement with the material must be kept alive or the class will soon share the lack of interest.

When non-verbal behaviour is not reinforcing meaning, therefore, it communicates instead the speaker's lack of involvement. Rather than being the message about the message, it becomes the message about the messenger.

Creating a serious atmosphere

Two dogs about to fight adopt rigid and alert postures. Cats stare at each other, motionless except for the slow movements of their tails. This extreme alertness is characteristic of many animals in aggressive confrontations and can also be observed in human beings. The behaviour is obviously very functional, as each must be prepared for an attack and this demands mutual vigilance.

In contrast to the relaxed and synchronised movements which accompany speech in an enthusiastic communication, speaking without bodily movements while steadily maintaining eye contact with the listener has overtones of aggressive threat. If the speech is also controlled and deliberate, the tension is increased. The dangers of showing signs of aggression have already been discussed but it is sometimes necessary to create a serious atmosphere and once the class are attending this can be achieved by speaking in such a way, without bodily movements. Heavy silences in extended pauses can create quite dramatic effects which every pupil senses. One student recounted how she was reprimanding her class with little success as they did not appear unduly concerned. She became aware that she was rubbing her left arm with her right hand as she spoke, and was therefore probably communicating her own insecurity. Moving to a more prominent position in the room, she continued speaking in a measured way but without moving her head or body and was surprised to find the class became very attentive.

One must beware of 'going over the top' by scowling and approaching to within inches of the victim's nose, because the credibility of such behaviour depends on one's capacity to follow up with an actual physical attack in the event of a continued challenge. This would hardly be appropriate even if one were fairly certain of winning. The object is to create an air of seriousness, so that one's words are heeded, rather than to invite a confrontation. In this respect it is safer to direct such behaviour towards a large group, rather than an individual.

Reading aloud

Teachers are often called upon to read aloud to the class, perhaps from a textbook or a pupil's written work. This calls for special skills, because reading aloud imposes a number of limitations on one's capacity to sustain a listener's attention. First of all, it is difficult to establish visual contact with individual pupils without considerable practice in reading ahead, and even then one must remember to leave a finger marking the place to which one's eyes must return. The best compromise many teachers can hope for is an occasional quick glance round to check that no one has quietly nodded off to sleep.

Another limitation is that one's movements are greatly restricted. If one hand is left free to gesture, it is not then available to mark the place on the page. Any movement of the head or hands can cause one to lose the place and interrupt the flow of the reading. Much of one's gaze is necessarily directed at the book, and one may therefore feel inhibited about displaying appropriate facial expressions for fear of looking bizarre: it is very difficult to sound convincingly happy, surprised or angry without producing the corresponding facial expression.

The major limitation imposed on the reader, however, is that he is not generating the thoughts and ideas he is expressing, but is merely reproducing words from a page. Any vocal variations must therefore be added as a conscious act, in order to clarify and extend the meaning. They are not spontaneously generated, so that one must read ahead to decide the author's intentions and how best to convey these to the listener. The major burden of clarifying meaning rests with vocal variations because gestures, facial expressions and eye contact are greatly reduced. Considerable practice is required to sustain the listener's attention, particularly if the text is uninspiring. When reading from a book it is often advisable to put a difficult story or explanation into one's own words either in place of, or in addition to, the text. This not only simplifies the language but also allows one to enhance the meaning with spontaneous non-verbal behaviour.

Children are themselves called upon to read aloud to the class and may do so in a 'flat' and uninteresting way, or give a repetitious and inappropriate variation on every sentence. Apart from giving them practice, and checking that they are able to read the words, reading aloud would seem to be better left to the teacher. It is, of course, easier to supervise the class if a pupil is reading but, if the reading is dull and uninteresting, supervision will be all the more necessary.

Responsiveness

Establishing eye contact with the listeners in a relaxed way not only contributes to an impression of being confident but also allows one to search for the reactions to one's teaching. Mehrabian found that there was an association between the apparent responsiveness of a speaker and the extent that he was seen as being persuasive: 'During persuasion, increased responsiveness to the listener is only natural since he is the primary focus of one's attention; however, it is interesting, too, that increased responsiveness also contributed to the perceived persuasive quality of a message.'

Enthusiastic teaching must use persuasion, and Mehrabian's work implies that if a teacher is searching for pupils' reactions, not only will he appear more responsive but the enthusiastic quality of the delivery is likely to be enhanced. It is notable that this readiness to respond to pupils' relevant and appropriate reactions contrasts with the apparent lack of responsiveness needed to create conditions in which that teaching can proceed (see p.22).

Associated with the notion of responsiveness is the teacher's sensitivity to the involvement of the group. Prior to the recording or broadcasting of a television show there is often an attempt to 'warm up' the studio audience so that they become more responsive, which in turn allows the performers to be more informal. A similar phenomenon occurs at parties where it may take some time (and alcohol) before people can relate to one another in a relaxed manner. It may also take time for a group to empathise with the mood of a speaker. Highly animated behaviour may enhance communication between two friends who are sharing the same mood or involvement with a subject, but it would seem totally incongruous from a person one had just met. In the same way a teacher who attempted to be very enthusiastic in the first moments of a lesson with new pupils would run the risk of drawing attention to his own behaviour, rather than to the information being conveyed. If one's involvement develops naturally in the course of introducing a topic it is more likely to be shared by the group.

Providing examples

Wherever possible one should provide relevant first-hand experiences as there is little point in, say, extolling the qualities of a piece of music without letting the pupils hear it. When I have the opportunity to teach the topic of 'Sustaining Attention', video-taped illustrations are essential if the group is to appreciate fully the points being made. Telling people about non-verbal behaviour is not enough, because when they later see an interesting speaker the great majority still fail to notice the way bodily movements relate to speech rhythms and meaning. It is necessary to take particular phrases and draw attention to the accompanying non-verbal behaviour in order to ensure that everyone understands. There is always an air of surprise as people first notice the relationship, even though they have already been told about it. Until they have the experience there is no real understanding. Only if this chapter has been read together with an attempt to observe the behaviours described will the reader be likely to appreciate the full significance of non-verbal behaviour in interpersonal communication.

This chapter has considered aspects of self-presentation which communicate one's feelings. It is this 'charismatic' quality which, to a large extent, enables a teacher almost to conduct the class through a range of emotional states from happy or excited to sad or serious. It is this capacity to capture pupils' attention which is a major basis for the teacher's authority.

5 Analysing Unwanted Behaviour

In the main, the reasons for unwanted behaviour are very straightforward. The child is not disturbed or showing symptoms of adverse home circumstances, nor has he some ulterior motive, conscious or unconscious, underlying his behaviour. He talks because he has something he wants to tell a friend at that moment; he runs in the corridor because he is in a hurry; he does something silly because it seems a good idea at the time and may relieve the boredom of a long day confined in the classroom.

In such cases, if the teacher happens to notice the child and takes some decisive action to stop the behaviour, the child responds favourably. This compliance, though delayed, reflects and restates the authority relationship. However, there are some children who receive frequent reprimands and sanctions yet still persist in unwanted behaviour and thereby bring the authority of the teacher into question.

It would be idealistic to suggest that a teacher can always prevent unwanted behaviour from pupils simply by keeping their interest. Sustaining attention effectively will certainly reduce the possibility of unwanted behaviour, but there are still bound to be occasions when it does occur. This chapter examines the sort of things that pupils do, or fail to do, which teachers feel is inappropriate behaviour at the time, and suggests some reasons for such behaviour.

If you want to know what pupil behaviours are inappropriate, ask a teacher. A group of teachers carried out a small exercise for me based on the questionnaire shown opposite. The school in which they worked was an urban comprehensive for eleven- to sixteen-year-olds, where standards of work and behaviour were rather better than average. The types of behaviours recorded in the survey reflected this in that they tended to be mild in character.

The pupil behaviour most frequently mentioned was, as one might expect, talking instead of listening or working. The more serious behaviours, where the pupil was sometimes referred to a senior member of staff, generally involved challenges to the teacher's authority. One teacher (Keith Glass) suggested we could categorise behaviours under three headings:

UNDERSTANDING 'DIFFICULT' BEHAVIOUR

The purpose of this exercise is to gain answers to three questions:

1 What do teachers regard as 'unwanted' pupil behaviours?
2 How do teachers *react* to unwanted pupil behaviours?
3 In what ways might we conceptualise unwanted pupil behaviours and teachers' reactions to them?

In the course of your teaching, or in any other interactions with pupils, you are asked to note your answers to the questions provided below, each time you notice or are involved in 'unwanted' pupil behaviour. Do this as soon after each 'event' as possible.

Could you please record *each event* on a separate sheet (i.e. your answers to Questions 1 to 4 below), and on an additional sheet your answers to Questions A to E.

Questions about each 'event'

1 What was the action, or lack of action, which drew your attention to the pupil(s)?
2 Did you react or change your behaviour in any way in response to the pupil's behaviour? Try to remember exactly what you said and/or did or felt.
3 What was the outcome of the action you took, or chose not to take?
4 Can you suggest *why* the pupil(s) should have acted as he/she/they did at that time? Try to avoid vague generalisations, e.g. 'deprived child' but rather suggest why the pupil chose to do what he did, rather than some other more appropriate behaviour such as doing what you wanted him to do.

Without conferring with other members of staff, can you in any way *categorise* the following:

A The unwanted pupil behaviours you have listed in your answers to 1.
B Your reactions listed in your answers to 2.
C The reasons for unwanted behaviour you have suggested in your answers to 4.
D Can you draw any conclusions about your own management of unwanted behaviour?
E Please comment, if you wish, on the exercise you have engaged in.

Thank you for your cooperation.

---

1 Those which violate the interests of the pupil concerned, such as failing to work or doing something dangerous to his own health or safety.
2 Those which violate the interests of the other pupils, such as distracting others from working, bullying and dangerous behaviour.
3 Those which violate the interests of the school or community, such

as challenging teachers' authority or failing to wear school uniform.

These are useful distinctions because teachers often use similar reasons to justify their reactions to unwanted behaviour:

1   'You won't stand a chance of passing the exam.' 'You could have fallen off and broken your neck.'

2   'You're not just wasting two minutes of his time, you're wasting two minutes of my teaching time, and that's two minutes of everybody's time so that's thirty-five lots of two minutes.'

3   'What will people think of this school if they see you dressed like that?'

Of course any one offence can fit into more than one category, but such a framework can provide a useful basis for staff and pupils to discuss written and unwritten rules.

It is not the object of recording and categorising unwanted behaviour to produce an exhaustive list of such acts, although it can be enlightening for teachers to carry it out and can indicate differences in the type of behaviour they notice. In any teaching situation which allows some pupil movement or involves potentially dangerous equipment, such as a science laboratory, gymnasium or craft room for example, the teacher will notice behaviour involving the safety of the pupils, such as running or using apparatus carelessly. The survey can also point out to a teacher what he might be failing to notice. If he only records the more serious offences, perhaps with one particular class, then he may be overlooking, or at least not realising, the significance of things like 'looking out of the window instead of writing'. It is often the case that serious misbehaviour occurs in a context of minor infractions such as general inattention, but the teacher has become resigned to the fact that he is unable to alter the situation. It might be that one class presents special problems for a number of teachers, and a list of observations might form the basis for discussion between the staff concerned (and perhaps between the staff and pupils in that class) as to how the situation can be improved.

If one particular pupil is the subject of a number of incidents with various teachers, then a much clearer picture can be built up of his behaviour during the day. Is he tending to avoid work, disrupt others or disobey teachers? Yes, will come the cynical reply from hardened campaigners, but a closer look at a pupil's behaviour may reveal some underlying pattern. Pik (1981) suggested a number of questions which might help in this respect.

– Does the pupil tend to have more confrontations with male or female staff?

– Are there more confrontations with junior staff and, if so, does the pupil's timetable show a large number of lessons with junior staff?

– Do there appear to be more confrontations during the more formal lessons or during the more 'free ranging' lessons such as art, PE and home economics, in which movement around the room, gym or kitchen is essential?

- Does the class size appear to be a significant factor?
- Is there a small group of his peers who might be providing a suitably provocative audience for the pupil in several of the classes during which confrontations take place?
- Is there a pattern of failure or difficulty with certain subjects which might be a contributing factor to confrontatins during these lessons? (Often signified by the days of the week on which the pupil poses difficulties or is absent from school.)
- With which teacher(s) does the pupil get on particularly well in and out of the classroom? (This person, even if he or she doesn't actually teach the child could be useful in a counselling role.)

When I was working as an educational psychologist I was asked to observe a seven-year-old boy who was disrupting the work of the other children to such an extent that the headteacher wondered whether the boy ought to be removed before the teacher resigned. I observed the boy with his class and, sure enough, he severely disrupted the work of those around him by hiding their pencils and books, scribbling over their work and walking around the room. During the course of the morning a pattern began to emerge. Firstly, he was not directing his disruptive acts towards the teacher. He obeyed instructions compliantly when told to move, or to stop doing something, but merely started again at the earliest opportunity. It was also interesting to see that the other children were quite tolerant and warm towards him, in spite of the fact that he may have just scribbled on or torn their work. Their reactions were similar to the way one would behave with handicapped or very young children, as if they were making allowances for his behaviour. It finally struck me that he had not once initiated any interaction with another pupil by *talking* to them, although they certainly spoke to him and he replied. This was significant as he had been receiving speech therapy for some time. One plausible explanation for his behaviour was that he had had a history of trying to talk to his peers without being understood, and had resorted to interacting with them in the way he did. He wanted to be part of their circle and to share in the attention, but had learned that his speech was inadequate. It must obviously have been very frustrating for him, and his disruptive behaviour was perhaps a product of his frustration.

In the School Council project on disturbed children (Wilson and Evans, 1980), a classification of behaviour disorders proved useful in relating various forms of treatment to particular types of disorder. It was found, for example, that many of the special schools and units using individual psychotherapy felt this to be a suitable treatment for pupils showing neurotic behaviours but only a few felt it helpful for conduct disorders. On the other hand, of the twenty-five schools and units using classroom management techniques derived from learning theory, only three felt this to be helpful with neurotic disorders. However, the difficulty still arises in making a clear assessment of the problem, assuming that the categories one is using have some construct validity. A careful record of what a child does may aid diagnosis. In attempting to categorise children's behaviour one must be aware of the danger of 'labelling' the child, as this can lead teachers to misinterpret what might be quite reasonable behaviour.

Three perspectives

It seems that when teachers are asked to speculate on the reasons for unwanted behaviour their reasons can be categorised in three distinct ways:

1   In terms of the *cause* of the behaviour, i.e. the past experience of the child which might predispose him towards certain behaviour, or temperamental factors.
2   In terms of the *pay-off* for the behaviour, i.e. what does the child gain by misbehaving?
3   In terms of the *contexts* in which unwanted behaviour is more likely to occur, i.e. the teacher's part in promoting unwanted behaviour.

1: Causes of unwanted behaviour

The association between inadequate or distorted early care of children and subsequent behaviour problems was highlighted by Bowlby's work in the mid-1950s on maternal deprivation. This prompted a great deal of research into the effects of separation and loss in a child's early experience, and the emphasis has now shifted away from the mother to the importance of a continuous and warm relationship with a mother figure. The effects of grossly distorted care, such as for children brought up in some institutions, were very pronounced and sometimes irreversible, and these children frequently had difficulty in establishing and sustaining relationships and suffered from lowered general ability. It now seems that these effects were due not only to the absence of warm continuous care with a mother figure, but also to insufficient sensory and intellectual stimulation. Today, children seldom suffer such extremes of privation, but there is little doubt that many are subject to distorted or inadequate care throughout childhood, due to a variety of family and economic difficulties. For example, one report (DES, 1978) noted that, in a first-year intake of one inner-city secondary school, the head of the family was unemployed in forty-four per cent of the cases, and thirty-four per cent had a mother or father suffering from chronic illness. Rutter *et al.* (1979), summarising the comparative study of children in an inner London borough and children on the Isle of Wight, concluded:

Family discord and disharmony, parental mental disorder, criminality in the parents, large family size and overcrowding in the home, admission of the child into care of the local authority and low occupational status were all associated with emotional or behavioural disturbance and/or reading retardation. As with previous studies there was ample evidence of the immense importance of family circumstances and family relationships in shaping children's development.

Adverse social and economic factors have long been associated with educational disadvantage and there is no reason to believe that matters have improved since that report.

The importance of environmental factors has, to a large extent, overshadowed the possibility that some children might be predisposed, genetically or congenitally, to experience learning and behaviour problems. Low general ability is, of course, a major factor in school failure, but specific learning difficulties may also affect a child's progress. The influence of inherent factors on certain types of reading problems has long been recognised and it may be that other subjects such as mathematics require specific abilities.

School failure and behaviour problems are strongly associated, but there is also evidence to suggest that some children may be more liable to develop behaviour problems due to temperamental factors. Thomas, Chess and Birch (1968) showed that the clinical cases in their longitudinal study were, as a group, 'characterised by an excessive frequency of either high or low activity, irregularity, withdrawal responses to novel stimuli, non-adaptability, high intensity, persistence and distractability'. They stressed the interaction of these traits with each other, and with environmental factors, as being crucial to the development of behaviour disorders.

Similarly, Mednick *et al.* (1987) found that the criminal records of adopted children showed a greater association with the records of their biological parents than the records of their adoptive parents implying an inherited factor in the susceptibility to commit crime. However, it is not possible to *predict* with certainty whether any particular child will develop behaviour problems, let alone the nature of those problems. Perhaps the unknown factor of inherited qualities determines how each child will interact with his environment, and the extent to which he can tolerate extremes of experience.

One of the comments I received from a teacher drew attention to a cycle of deprivation in which many children seem trapped:

> The boy has a number of problems in the home known to many staff. Attendance is infrequent and motivation is poor. Consequently his achievements are low and this does little to improve his motivation. His misbehaviour is an attempt to seek attention from the teacher and other pupils, to break the tedium.

It is obviously crucial to bear these circumstances in mind when consideration is being given to offering special educational help, removing a child into care or suggesting residential schooling, but knowledge of them gives little practical guidance to the teacher on how to cope with the behaviour in the most effective way.

It is not within most teachers' power to compensate for very adverse home circumstances, even if they are eager to help. In primary schools, where there is prolonged contact with the same group of children, it is difficult to attend to one child for any length of time in a large class. In secondary schools, teachers have limited contact with whole classes, let alone individual pupils. Even when parents are apparently contributing to their child's problems, they are sometimes incapable of changing the situation because of emotional and economic problems. I saw one eight-year-old boy who had been referred for persistent stealing in school and at home. He could not be left for a minute in reach of anyone's property, and had even entered a neighbour's house and stolen jewellery. Hoarding food and stealing in young children can sometimes be a symptom of early lack of affection, and it seemed likely that this might be a significant feature in the boy's behaviour. His mother said that she had never been able to show her son any physical affection, because she could not bear to be touched by anyone. She did not even feel able to put her arm around him. At such a late stage, some children find great difficulty anyway in accepting affection, so whether or not this would have helped was by then probably purely academic.

What, then, can teachers do when faced with pupils who suffer from adverse home circumstances? Clearly they will try to help by giving as much time and personal attention as possible. It is unlikely, though, that one will be able to bring about a lasting change in attitude in a deviant pupil by concerning oneself with his problems at the expense of actually teaching him. We may be aware that the father is in prison and the mother has no time for the child, and our hope is that, by understanding his problems and developing a relationship with him, he may feel less inclined to misbehave and will improve his attitude to work. But if we fail to teach him anything, he will have yet another problem. If we are to earn a child's respect or thanks, or if a relationship is to develop, it will probably be more as a result of our having taught him something. In this respect teaching is caring.

Children, like some adults, sometimes take advantage of their handicaps. I remember one boy who was short-sighted and who certainly did have a problem which could affect his progress, but the teacher suggested he used this as an excuse for doing very little work. I came across a similar instance when supervising a student on teaching practice. The first-year class had been set to work on a piece of creative writing, but one boy was spending most of his time looking out of the window at a nearby football match. I picked up his exercise book and pointed out that he had written twenty words in as many minutes, and that eight of those were incorrectly spelt. 'Ah yes, sir,' he announced, 'That's my problem.' Someone had probably mentioned that he had a spelling problem and, as far as he was concerned, this was his passport to educational immunity. What he did not realise, or chose to ignore, was that *greater* effort is called for from those who suffer the disadvantages of a disability.

In many cases a child obviously suffers from an educational or social disadvantage, but there is a danger that he will regard his problems as inevitable and insurmountable. Teachers must always encourage children to take responsibility for their own development, rather than regard themselves as passive victims of circumstance. We have, perhaps, been encouraged to regard a child's psychological integrity as far more fragile than it really is.

A causal approach should, therefore, take into account factors like previous experience, intelligence, personality characteristics and physical condition in attempting to explain why certain children persistently misbehave. This information can enable teachers to provide appropriate work and remedial help, which could have an indirect effect on the pupil's conduct.

More immediate experience can also affect children's behaviour. A bout of untypical misbehaviour, or a decline in the standard of work, might well be symptoms of some temporary trauma or set-back in the home or with friends. A child obviously needs support and understanding at a time of crisis, and teachers should be sensitive to sudden changes of work and behaviour as these might be the only indications that something is wrong.

Disagreements also arise between pupils in school which necessitate the teacher's intervention but these are rather different from the unwanted behaviour discussed so far. They occur fairly frequently and can sometimes impose a great deal of stress, particularly for those pupils who are the objects of bullying. It is probably better that pupils as well as teachers should take responsibility for keeping the peace, as arguments and fights usually take place well out of sight of the staff.

To summarise, therefore, a knowledge of relevant factors in a child's background can contribute to an understanding of the problems faced by the child. Such knowledge, however, does not necessarily leave one any wiser about treatment. In fact a sympathetic teacher may unwittingly confirm to a child his inadequacies by too readily accepting lower standards of work and behaviour so that his problems are compounded. Similarly an unsympathetic and coercive regime may further alienate the pupil. The question that must be addressed is 'In what ways can schools help to overcome the various disadvantages suffered by some children?' As Galloway *et al.* (1982) noted:

> We are not saying that disadvantaged homes and delinquent neighbourhoods have no effect on pupils' behaviour at school. That would be absurd. We *are* saying that our own research confirms the evidence of other research teams in emphasising the school's own influence over its pupils' behaviour.

It might be more fruitful, in terms of suggesting measures which teachers might take to help children, to examine the possible ways in which unwanted behaviour may be reinforced in school.

2: Pay-offs or rewards for unwanted behaviour

A practical approach is to consider what a child might gain from misbehaving: What is the *reward*? It is important to do this because teachers may unwittingly be encouraging the very behaviour they wish to remove. As with the 'causes', one can never be certain that any particular event is acting as a reward, but one can speculate that some of the more likely motives for unwanted behaviour are attention seeking from teachers and peers, creating excitement, malicious teasing of teachers, and avoiding work.

Attention seeking

A common explanation offered for unwanted behaviour is that the child is attention seeking, probably to compensate for a lack of parental care, and there is no doubt that in some cases this could be valid.

I remember observing a six-year-old boy who had been referred to the Schools' Psychological Service. The class were engaged in individual and group activities when the teacher called them around her so that she could have a session on 'telling the time'. Sure enough, the boy took no notice of her but stayed at the back of the room and fiddled with some milk bottles. The teacher told him to leave them and come and join the others, but he showed no reaction to her having spoken. After several similar fruitless attempts, she told him that if he came quickly, he could turn the hands of the clock she was using. His response was immediate and he spent the session on her lap, at the centre of attention of the class. The teacher had not rewarded the fact that he had done as he was told, as everyone else had gathered round her long before him. She had rewarded the fact that he had initially stayed away, and so he was learning that disobedience can bring rewards. Parents often reward pestering and whining from their children in the same way, by giving the child what he wants or an acceptable alternative. They may try to divert the child's attention from the desired object by offering some other interesting activity, but this only has the same effect in that it will not reduce future pestering, but simply stops the present bout.

Rewarding unhelpful behaviour is most likely to occur at the infant stage, when teachers may know of genuine difficulties in home circumstances and therefore 'make allowances' for children's behaviour in an attempt to compensate for, or at least not aggravate, their problems. However, they are certainly not helping by rewarding misbehaviour. Children must learn to get the attention they need by behaving well.

Another frequent practice which can serve as a reward for some children is the individual 'Dutch uncle' chat with the teacher or headteacher. Following some misbehaviour the teacher will try to make the child appreciate the error of his ways, or 'see reason' by accepting the teacher's point of view. The hope is that such individual 'counselling' will help with his underlying problems. This ensures individual attention for as long as one is presenting a problem and in some cases, particularly at a time of crisis, it may be beneficial. If it continues to occur only as a result of bad behaviour, however, or if the child's problems form the main subject of the talk, there is a real danger of maintaining the misbehaviour. It is unlikely that many pupils of secondary school age regard a private 'inquest' with a teacher as rewarding, but they probably find it preferable to detention or some other sanction. With these children it would probably not be a factor in the maintenance of the behaviour, but it would be unlikely to do much to change it.

Teacher attention does not necessarily increase the behaviour at which it is directed. Even if the child originally learns to misbehave in order to get positive or rewarding attention, as he grows older he is more likely to find that the sort of attention he gets from the teacher can be far from rewarding. No one can really like being belittled in front of his peers for long, being shouted at, given extra work or, as was the case until recently, caned. To suggest that this type of attention will sustain misbehaviour is certainly contrary to what Skinnerian learning theory would predict, although it is sometimes suggested that any attention is better than none. It is more likely that the child tolerates the risk of such treatment because he is gaining other benefits or, as we shall see later, because he does not feel that he is the victim when the teacher becomes annoyed.

If teachers are in the habit of giving attention to children who have misbehaved, then they should be sure that their attention is having the desired effect. Whether they are attempting to be frightening, understanding or sarcastic, it may be that these measures are in fact perpetuating the behaviour they are intended to curb. In the lesson on 'telling the time', it would probably have been better in the long run to reward the first child who was ready to begin, by letting him turn the hands of the clock, and to have made the session as lively and interesting as possible, letting other children also take an active part. The boy at the back of the class would soon have become bored with the milk bottles and would have had to decide whether to join the group quietly or disrupt it, perhaps by launching a bottle through the window. This may seem an extreme reaction, but if one cuts off attention in this way, the child's behaviour will deteriorate further in order to regain attention, assuming that was his original objective. The teacher is then forced to notice, and the child's misbehaviour is aggravated. It is essential, therefore, to anticipate an escalation and be prepared to meet it.

Attention seeking from peers is common, particularly at the secondary stage. Many adolescents are very concerned to be accepted by their fellow pupils and this can give rise to a wide range of behaviour. On the positive side, if a group of friends have good attitudes towards school and high academic aspirations, effort and success will gain favourable acclaim; but if the attitudes are anti-school, such as those outlined by Hargreaves (1967), then failure to produce work or disobedience to teachers will meet with peer group approval. However, the norms and values of groups can vary from day to day, as can the membership of those groups. Similarly, rudeness towards one teacher may receive open approval from fellow-pupils, whereas with another well-liked teacher, support might not be forthcoming.

One should be aware of the pressure on a pupil to maintain relationships with friends, which will entail behaving in ways he feels the group will value, or giving approval to similar behaviour by others. If he finds himself in a confrontation with a teacher, he will not want to lose face by backing down in front of his friends, but could gain a good deal of prestige if he is seen to flout the teacher's authority. It is always safer, therefore, to postpone such battles until they can be dealt with privately, when peer group pressure will be less evident.

If the school organisation is sufficiently flexible to split up groups of disruptive pupils into different classes, this can leave a 'performer' without his audience. A more extreme effect is achieved by moving a pupil to another school. Most teachers have experienced the abrupt and welcome change of behaviour when a key 'deviant' is absent, though it may be that another will emerge to take on the role.

Various researchers, particularly in the field of behaviour modification, have attempted to manipulate peer group approval by rewarding the whole class for the good behaviour of one member. For instance, the class might be allowed extra games if a certain child avoids getting into trouble for a specified time. In this way the class are discouraged from approving his bad behaviour as they will suffer as a result, and the deviant pupil has the opportunity to earn group approval by acceptable behaviour. Some schools and units for children with behaviour disorders run token economy schemes whereby, when a boy behaves in an unacceptable way, every member of his group or house forfeits tokens which could otherwise be exchanged for goods or privileges. Group reprisals against one unfortunate member are discouraged by the same pressure in that they would all lose further tokens. Such approaches have also been used successfully in normal day school settings, though the class teacher is usually given support and advice (Coulby and Harper, 1985).

Teachers sometimes try to ignore mild unwanted behaviour, in accordance with the principles of learning theory, but find that other pupils provide the necessary reinforcement. This can be by actively supporting the culprit, by laughing or calling out suitable remarks, or by apparently supporting the teacher with remarks like 'Please, Miss,

Johnny's out of his seat again.' In the latter case the informant may be seeking teacher approval, but it would probably be preferable to tell him to get on with his own work rather than thank him for his help. There are some less obvious examples of seeking peer group attention, as in the case of the boy with a speech difficulty mentioned earlier (p.77), who disrupted other children's work apparently as a substitute for talking to them, but these are exceptional.

As pupils progress into adolescence it becomes more difficult for teachers to deal with anti-school groups, because as teachers they are representatives of the general authority which is being challenged. Some younger teachers may be able to develop good relationships with the more deviant groups if their appearance and manner is very informal, but they run the risk of being frowned on by colleagues, who may feel that they avoid confrontations only by failing to uphold standards of work and behaviour. One can minimise the formation of deviant groups by avoiding rigid streaming or any other organisation which throws together potentially difficult children unless they receive specialised help. Regrettably, however, some teachers in inner-city areas would justifiably feel that most of their pupils were potentially difficult.

Causing excitement

Mills (1975) has proposed an interesting theory which offers an explanation for a wide range of unusual behaviour from children. His suggestion is that in order to cope with the various problems and stresses of life, the arousal level of the brain is increased so that it functions more efficiently. If the stresses are within normal limits for the individual, the arousal level of the brain drops during sleep, but if there are difficult problems to cope with, the brain becomes highly aroused during the day and does not recover its normal resting level during sleep. The person therefore wakes in the early hours of the morning and worries over the problems of the day to come, usually to little effect. Although he is too aroused to sleep, he is not sufficiently aroused to cope with making difficult decisions, and this can cause him to feel very depressed because he can see no way out of the problems which are depriving him of his rest.

Mills cites research showing that, with prolonged periods of stress or excitement, there is a build-up of an underlying depression which is manifest when the arousal of the brain lowers. The person therefore seeks excitement to ward off the feelings of depression. Mills suggests there are alternative ways of increasing the arousal level of the brain, such as by not eating, and offers this theory to account for the illness annorexia nervosa.

The main concern for Mills is with those people who are depressed because they are unable to cope with the problems in their lives, but he also suggests that many children are subject to considerable stress in their homes. Perhaps the parents quarrel frequently and the children may have no opportunity for quiet and privacy. The mother may be tired and often hit out or scream at them. Perhaps when they watch television, which they tend to do for long periods of time, they choose the exciting programmes and so maintain high levels of arousal. When such a child is at school his lessons probably seem very 'flat' in comparison, because he is geared up or conditioned to a high degree of stimulation. Mills suggests that the pupil therefore actually tries to create excitement, which usually involves behaving illicitly. The risk of being caught and punished, which normally acts as a deterrent, would only encourage such a child. In fact without that risk his action would be pointless:

> Nowadays a number of children and young people have found that mild depression may be overcome by doing something exciting. This may be going to a pop concert with music at pain-producing intensity: it may be challenging authority at home or at school or it may involve stealing or other law breaking activities. The more depressed they are, the more exciting the challenge has to be to mask their depression. Many of these young people have described the progressive increase in devilment that is necessary to stop feeling depressed. Producing an intense disturbance in class, in which the other children soon become involved, is a favourite and effective mechanism.

We all seek some excitement in our lives, though most of us learn to achieve it in socially acceptable ways. Some choose sports which are either competitive or have an element of danger, others find their business provides sufficient risks or competition. Gambling is another form of excitement, and an illicit love affair is attractive partly because it is illicit. Most people now enjoy excitement vicariously, from television and films, without any actual risk involved, but Mills' theory suggests that all this need not remain a static or balanced process, with different people requiring different levels of excitement in their lives. It is a dynamic process, such that an increasing diet of excitement can, up to a point, feed one's need for further stimulation to the extent that one tries to create more. A child, through no fault of his own necessarily, could be continually subjected to a highly stimulating environment in the home and so become over-aroused. This would develop a compulsion for dangerous and forbidden behaviour, so that school life becomes as exciting as life at home.

When a teacher reacts emotionally to unwanted behaviour he may believe that the experience will be unpleasant for the pupil, but in fact he could be taking a leading role in the drama which the pupil is trying to create. Instead it would be better to attempt to appear relaxed and unruffled, neither smug nor insecure in whatever action he takes. Advocates of behaviour modification would suggest trying to ignore the child who is misbehaving, but, as mentioned earlier, it is difficult to stop other pupils attending. The idea of 'time-out' periods when the behaviour is too disruptive or dangerous to ignore, however, is quite useful.

'Time-out' entails removing the child from the class in a quiet, unemotional way, to a room where he has nothing to do at all. He must be supervised, though not spoken to, and this may present problems of staffing in some schools. In junior schools the headteacher's room will suffice, provided no one takes any notice of the pupil. After about ten minutes or so the child should be returned to the classroom without comment, and the teacher should speak to him on the first occasion he does something right, not mentioning the events leading to his removal.

The crucial factor in the effectiveness of this approach is probably the calm attitude which the teacher conveys. Pupils are more usually removed from the room as a last resort after warnings and reprimands, and so it is often an emotional and exciting affair. In contrast, if the child is removed quietly before he has created any excitement to a place which he finds even more boring than the classroom, he will learn that unwanted behaviour is not always effective in enlivening the situation. When he is returned to the classroom he is likely to find it relatively stimulating compared with the time-out period and may therefore behave better. Some schools set aside a classroom where children from any group can be sent to work under the supervision of a teacher for an extended period of time, and this would seem to have a similar effect.

The difficulty arises for some teachers in getting the child to leave the classroom without actually throwing him out. Hamblin *et al.* (1971) describe one difficult boy whom they had to restrain from leaving the time-out room, and then found that this treatment did not improve his behaviour. (This exciting experience could be its own reward according to Mills' theory.) They therefore allowed him to leave the room and wander around the school, but not to return to his class until he had willingly served his ten minutes back in the time-out room. They found this much more effective, but one wonders what there was to prevent the boy from damaging school property, wandering back into his room or leaving the school premises entirely. Against a really determined child there would seem to be little alternative to physical force, but there is less likelihood of resistance if the child is removed in an unthreatening manner before an emotional confrontation and battle of wills has arisen.

The theory associating high arousal with deviant behaviour is attractive, though it does not explain why some children find legitimate means of creating excitement and other behave anti-socially. It does, however, reinforce the points which were made earlier about the need to present an interesting and varied lesson and to develop the skills of enthusiastic teaching. If teachers can make school life more stimulating, the difficult child will not only have less need to make his own excitement, but will also find it harder to involve others in his schemes.

Malicious teasing

Alison, a thirteen-year-old, tells of an incident with her teacher, Mr

Baker: 'I once threw something on to his desk. He wasn't sure who had thrown it. He didn't do anything. He just glared at me. I like getting him stewed up. I don't know why. It's fun, but sometimes he frightens me too.' (Wragg and Wood, 1984b)

It may come as no surprise to some that children should actually enjoy annoying teachers, and this idea, as put forward by Hamblin *et al.* (1971), seems to offer a plausible explanation for some instances of misbehaviour. They suggest that a great deal of children's unhelpful or annoying behaviour can be regarded as a form of malicious teasing whereby they engage in a game of 'Let's get the teacher'. They describe a group of five extraordinarily aggressive four-year-old boys referred to their laboratory by local psychiatrists and social workers. All had been diagnosed as hyperactive and none had responded to amphetamine therapy. Hamblin provided the group with a trained teacher and, after the eighth day, was recording an average of 150 sequences of aggression per day, which included such extreme behaviour as knocking over the record player and throwing chairs at the teacher. Hamblin comments on the way the situation developed:

> What she [the teacher] did not realise is that she had inadvertently structured an exchange where she consistently reinforced aggression. First, as noted, whenever she fought with them she always lost. Second, more subtly, she reinforced their aggressive pattern by giving it serious attention – by looking, talking, scolding, cajoling, becoming angry, even striking back. These boys were playing a teasing game called 'Get the Teacher'. The more she showed that she was bothered by their behaviour, the better they seemed to like it and the further they went.

Clearly, although the teacher was dispensing what might be considered fairly aversive treatment for most four-year-olds, she was the real victim in the exchanges.

The objective of malicious teasing, therefore, is to annoy and upset another individual by mental rather than physical cruelty. It is often a shared 'sport' among children so that a number of them will 'gang up' on one individual. The victim need not be weaker or smaller than others; indeed, there is probably an added pleasure in seeing someone stronger than you under your power, albeit a shared power.

If the teacher is not careful in his first meetings with children, he can soon find himself the victim of malicious teasing. It may start in the form of apparently innocent questions and comments which delay the progress of the lesson, but can develop into deliberate disobedience calculated to enrage the teacher. When I first taught at a comprehensive school the headteacher asked the staff to be more vigilant about pupils' conduct around the school, particularly concerning the amount of litter on the premises. As I walked across the playground a group of 'anti-school' fifteen-year-old boys were standing nearby and one threw some paper on the ground. I walked over and, in what I thought was a reasonable manner, asked him to pick it up and put it in the bin. I felt the tension from the group immediately, as they waited to see what he would do: 'I didn't drop it ... sir', the last word being slipped in to pay lip-service to my position, at the same time as showing contempt for it. He was immediately supported by his friend apparently providing an impregnable alibi. 'That's right, sir, he never dropped it. We've been wiv' im all the time and he never dropped nuffin. Did you see him drop anyfin, Steve?' Steve immediately complied: 'No, we was just standing 'ere talkin. Someone else must 'ave dropped it before we come 'ere.' They had all immediately sensed the game. It wasn't anything to do with waste paper being picked up or not, it was a battle between them and teachers. They were telling me, within the rules of teacher-pupil relationships, to go jump in the river. At that stage in my teaching career, challenges were never to be refused. I ignored the others and looked straight at the first boy. 'I saw you drop the paper, but it's not important whether you did or not, I'm telling you to pick it up now.' After a brief contemptuous pause he reluctantly bent down and picked up the paper. I held my hand out for him to pass it to me, but in a sudden moment of defiance he passed it to his friend. Before I realised what I was doing, I had clipped him across the side of the head with my outstretched hand. He and his friend who had the paper were outraged and erupted into threats of 'going to the courts' and swore to get me 'slung out', as they had witnessed my assault. I immediately took the two main offenders to the headteacher, where they made their accusations, and he had the good sense to cane them both.

No more was heard of the matter, but in many ways I was lucky. I didn't hit him harder, they didn't hit me back, the headteacher backed me up, and their parents presumably didn't back them up. I should not have hit a pupil, as the matter could so easily have leaped out of control. Although I had demonstrated my power they would probably have been confirmed in their anti-school attitudes. I say probably because after that event the main culprit always gave me a cheery 'mornin', sir', which never ceased to amaze me and I still can't see why.

Here was an example of a typical confrontation forced by the pupils, where the only motive seemed to be to challenge the authority of the teacher in a form of malicious teasing, not because he was unfair or wrong, but because he was in authority. Corporal punishment is now illegal in schools and we are compelled to think of better ways of handling such incidents (see p.138). Picking up the paper was such an insignificant act but I believed that my authority rested on the boy's compliance so I immediately resorted to a show of power.

Challenging authority is a common motive for misbehaviour, particularly among anti-school adolescents, and one can suggest many reasons why such attitudes may have developed. Perhaps the pupils are frustrated by failure and are hitting back at the system which they consider responsible. It might be an attempt to establish their individuality by challenging anyone in authority, and there are those who would regard it as a form of self-expression. Be that as it may, unless the teacher is very careful, he can be left frustrated by his own impotence and unable to exert any control over the culprits, which renders him ineffective as their teacher.

Malicious teasing is only successful if the victim is left annoyed, upset and frustrated. If an emotional response is not forthcoming then the teasing may escalate at first but, if this in turn fails, the offenders usually begin to feel very uncomfortable. From the teacher's point of view, the most successful outcome would be one where the pupils did as they were told without the satisfaction of seeing the teacher annoyed, and which maintained a good working relationship.

It follows, then, that in giving directions a teacher should not show any signs of tension, even if there is obvious reluctance or aggression from the pupils. The aim should be to sustain a calm atmosphere, without giving way to unreasonable pressure. If pupils are obviously determined to challenge the teacher from the outset, it is not helpful to react aggressively, as this implies that their challenge is realistic and therefore invites an escalation. Relaxed behaviour is certainly important in avoiding potential confrontations, as it offers no reinforcement to malicious teasing, so if one doesn't feel relaxed then at least one must try to appear so. In order to do this it is helpful to keep matters in a low key, or in the words of Gnagey (1975): 'Don't make a Federal case out of it!'

If the teacher knows what steps he intends to take if a pupil refuses to follow instructions, this will also help reduce the possibility of an emotional outburst. It is when one doesn't know what to do next that one either shows signs of anxiety or, perhaps to disguise this, becomes aggressive in an attempt to force the pupil into submission. Behaviour modification theory is useful in this respect, as it provides the teacher with a clear course of action requiring a non-emotional interaction.

Avoiding work

Ideally one should always derive pleasure from work, but this does not mean that work can be pleasurable all the time. Children have a very clear idea of what work is, perhaps because their level of mastery is low, so that they have less opportunity to derive satisfaction from their efforts or possibly because they possess what Ausubel (1968) described as 'the typical human proclivity towards procrastination and aversion to sustained, regular and disciplined work'. Any parents who have tried to make their children practise a musical instrument regularly will know what he means. It is not necessarily that children lack interest in the subject, but often that the effort of mastering a difficult skill, or of ordering their thoughts to produce a piece of written work, causes them to delay beginning the task. Almost always, talking about a subject is preferable to writing about it, and it is worth remembering that nearly every day of their school lives children have to produce written work in some form or other. The topic can be fascinating, the resources provided can be stimulating, the class visit can bring first-hand experience and the discussion can enlighten them to others' views, but the crunch still comes when they have to put pen to paper. Gannaway (1976) compiled a 'popularity table' of pupil activities, based on statements and comments from pupils, and suggested that writing was often synonymous with work: 'Writing is not only bottom of the table, but it is also the only activity that is always referred to as "work". A distinction is commonly drawn between writing and talking, the former being work and the latter being not work.' It is some consolation that the full onset of the affliction is delayed until adolescence, giving junior school teachers a somewhat rosy view of children's capacities or their own powers of motivation.

Buzan (1971) vividly describes what must be a fairly universal experience for students as they settle down to private study:

> Having decided to study on a certain evening the student will spend approximately five to ten minutes tidying and 'getting ready' his desk, making sure that everything is in the right place before he starts. Just as he is about to sit down, however, he will 'remember' that there is an important telephone call that he has to make and that if he doesn't make it he will be ill-at-ease during the study period. He makes the call (which is seldom brief!) and returns to his desk where he again adjusts the position of the study book, perhaps opens it and then suddenly 'remembers' that there is a television programme he was particularly interested in, so he goes to the next room to check the television schedules. Sure enough it begins in fifteen minutes! As fifteen minutes is not enough time to commence studying he decides to wait until after the programme.

We no doubt differ in our capacities to overcome this inertia; or, putting it another way, some people are lazier than others.

These feelings are apparently not confined solely to the human species. An American psychologist, giving an account of the progress which had been made in the remarkable work of teaching monkeys to use sign language, described how, when it was time for a lesson on learning new signs, one monkey regularly gave the sign for 'Me tired'. We all know that feeling!

It is true that children don't have to fool around to avoid work. They can simply sit and daydream and, when challenged by the teacher as to why they have done so little work, they offer a plausible excuse: 'Please Miss, I don't understand what we're doing' or 'I carn finka nuffin'. The pupil will not admit that he doesn't understand because his daydream started half-way through your enthusiastic explanation, or that the last thing he intended to think about was his work. However, both excuses sometimes appeal to the professional expertise of the dedicated and concerned, not to say gullible and inexperienced, teacher: 'Well, why didn't you ask me then, instead of just sitting there doing nothing?' There lies the answer, because if the teacher usually responds to pupils' questions in a reasonable way, then one can only assume that the child was not interested in help.

Why is it then that some children do not merely passively avoid work but creat a nuisance as well? One reason is that they may find it very boring just to sit and do nothing. Although they don't want to make the effort to work, they can't tolerate the lack of activity, and so at the very least they will occupy themselves by reading a comic or scribbling the name of their latest idol framed in a loving heart. As has already been discussed, some children may have a compulsive need for a degree of excitement in their environment and these would be likely to produce more disruptive behaviour.

It is disconcerting for a child to see his friends working when he doesn't want to make the effort. Either the child must decide to knuckle down and not be the odd one out, or he must contrive to stop them working. A case of 'If you can't join them, beat them!' There is also a chance that the teacher will then reprimand the class rather than the individual.

One way that the teacher will be more likely to overcome work avoidance is to make his minimum requirements clear to the class. He should let them know how much time remains for them to be working and relate this to the amount of work he expects. For instance, a mathematics lesson might proceed as follows. The teacher has just worked an example on the board and is addressing the class: 'As there are no more questions, I assume you all understood the method. Now you have twenty-five minutes left for this lesson, and I want you all to copy the example down in your books and continue with the exercise. Each question shouldn't take more than four minutes, so I'll expect everyone to have completed at least five questions as well as the example. If you can't manage them you can finish off at twelve o'clock in my room. I'll collect the books at the end of the lesson.' Every pupil knows what is expected of him, and that it is not unreasonable. They also know what will happen if they fail to complete the five questions: they lose some of their lunch hour (incidentally, so will the teacher, but he must be prepared for this). The children also realise that he will see their books and find out if they have, in fact, done the work. It is vital to check on this as if one fails to discover a culprit, credibility is lost.

It is not always necessary to collect the work if one is too busy, as pupils can exchange books and mark the work at the end of the lesson. If children's work is regularly taken in and marked, the teacher can ensure that poor or otherwise inadequate work is quickly rectified by the child. Obviously, if the work had been poorly done by the majority of the class this could indicate that the teaching was at fault, but a child should not learn that any rubbish he cares to present will be accepted. Good work habits are not easy to establish with some children, and the teacher must be consistent, organised and, most of all, persistent in his approach. In short, his own work habits must be above reproach. If one does tell a child to come back at the lunch hour to complete some work, it is essential not to forget. If necessary, one should get into the habit of writing down these details in a book, and refer to it regularly.

It is important to avoid a confrontation when telling a pupil that he will be expected to complete the work in his own time. It must not seem to him that he is being punished for his failure to work, but merely that he obviously needs more time to do it properly. At the end of the lesson, when he offers his excuses about not understanding, having no ideas or losing his pencil, the teacher has no need to remonstrate with him or discuss the validity of his reasons. All he has to do is show interest only in the work, or lack of it: 'You've only managed two, I see. Never mind, you can finish the other three at twelve o'clock.' If the work was an essay for which the child pleaded a lack of ideas then one might say: 'Yes, you haven't managed to think of a great deal. Try to think of some ideas before you come at twelve o'clock, or it may take you rather a long time to do the two sides of work.'

One must convey to the child, by one's attitude, that it is inevitable that the work will be completed, even in the event of a nuclear explosion, as it is important for his future progress. He must feel the teacher has his interests at heart and is not merely being vindictive; in this way he is less likely to refuse and provoke a confrontation.

If the child knows he will lose his free time later, he will be more likely to ask for help if he genuinely doesn't understand. The whole approach depends for its success on the teacher's ability to identify those children who fail to meet the goal set, and to persist until they do the work. If the child clearly tries hard during the extra time but achieves little, then this provides the opportunity for the teacher to give individual help, so he should not feel guilty about detaining someone who may have been trying hard during the lesson. If he is satisfied that certain children really do have difficulty in keeping up with the rest of the class, he can quietly tell them what they are expected to achieve after having spoken to the whole class.

When the goals set are realistic this will discourage pupils from time-wasting or misbehaving, and it will allow the teacher to ignore such behaviour as long as those children who want to work are able to. If some children have been fooling around, yet have still managed to do the work, then either more should have been set or the troublemakers are bright but not interested. If this is the case one may have to resort to sanctions to discourage the behaviour, as well as trying to stimulate the children's interest. In my experience, setting a minimum target does not discourage children who are keen from doing more work. They often try to double or treble the amount if they can.

When one does not wish to set the whole class a minimum target, it is still possible to do this with pupils who are wasting time in the course of the lesson. The teacher should tell them he will be looking at their work again in ten or fifteen minutes, and specify what they should do during that time. He must also make clear what the consequences are for failing to meet the target. Again, it is vital not to forget to go back at the right time.

Sometimes most of the children will attempt to divert the teacher from getting on with the lesson in a form of mass work avoidance, but this is usually quite good-natured if it does not happen too often. I remember at my school if we could possibly bring up the subject of the last war with one of our teachers, he could not resist recounting his experiences to us. We would attend avidly, asking the most relevant questions, and offering our own second-hand experiences if he seemed to be flagging. In this way we would avoid the best part of the lesson and feel triumphant. This was good-natured on our part, and I am sure that he allowed us the occasional interludes from his subject when it became a little tedious, as he usually ensured that everyone worked hard.

Nevertheless it is often very difficult, or impossible, to ensure that every child does sufficient work in each lesson. With large classes, and methods which sometimes involve children working on different material at different rates, it is difficult enough keeping track of what a child is supposed to be doing, let alone ensuring they have done a reasonable amount. Some teachers go to elaborate lengths to record the progress of children's work, and this is time well spent because in individual learning it is too easy for pupils to do very little.

When in doubt, one should demand a little more from the child than he can comfortably do, as, if he never has to make a real effort he is likely to lose interest. Teachers sometimes praise work which may have entailed little effort from the child, in the hope that he will feel encouraged to work harder. However, Festinger (1961) pointed out that success without effort will probably decrease interest and motivation. It is therefore wiser to be sure that the child has made some effort before giving praise, for, as Festinger noted after reviewing experiments on animal and human motivation: 'Rats and people come to love the things for which they have suffered.'

The task for teachers then is to persuade children to suffer willingly in the hope that they will ultimately gain satisfaction from their efforts. It should always be easier for a pupil to do the work than to avoid it.

3: Contexts for unwanted behaviour

In a questionnaire exercise I conducted with teachers, many of them realised their own responsibility for creating the circumstances in which unwanted behaviour would be more likely to occur: 'I feel the fault is mine – I should create more interest in the pupils' and 'My approach to the lesson may not have been very imaginative and stimulating – but I don't expect that every lesson can be so'. As well as taking the lesson as a whole and making an overall judgment such as 'uninteresting', one can identify circumstances during the lesson which could contribute to unwanted behaviour.

Kounin (1970) deals with what he calls *movement management*, which involves the skills of initiating an activity, directing pupils through it and sustaining their attention, and then successfully terminating it. Movement management concerns the pace and flow of one type of activity to another, such as from listening to the teacher to writing in books or carrying out an experiment. He distinguishes two aspects of movement management: *momentum* and *smoothness*.

Momentum

This is the liveliness and pace with which a lesson progresses. The comments made in Chapter 4 would be relevant here, but Kounin's approach is to look for what he terms *slowdowns*, which prevent or interrupt the momentum of a lesson. Slowdowns can be caused by *overdwelling* – spending a disproportionate amount of time on an inappropriate subject – or by *fragmentation* – dealing with individuals one at a time when one ought to be dealing with the whole group.

If the teacher spends too much time dealing with a minor aspect of a topic, particularly if the majority of pupils have already grasped the point, or if the aspect is somewhat irrelevant and uninteresting, this will cause a slowdown in momentum. Kounin calls this *actone overdwelling*. Similarly, *behaviour overdwelling* refers to excessive nagging or reprimanding of a pupil in the course of a lesson (see p.99), and the reaction in the pupils would be one of 'Doesn't he go on!' (In my experience, on these occasions there is also an absence of any direct constructive action, such as giving a sanction.) The teacher should always be looking for the pupils' reactions to what is being said or done, because signs of disinterest or other unwanted behaviour will indicate that the momentum of a lesson is being lost.

'Fragmentation' entails the teacher dealing with individual pupils when it would be more appropriate to deal with the whole group. The effect is to keep the rest of the class waiting unnecessarily. Teachers of drama and games are well aware of the importance of involving the majority of the children in an activity, rather than leaving them to be passive spectators for any length of time. The same principle applies in class teaching when, for example, a line of children wait for their work to be marked before they proceed further. Most teachers avoid such obvious 'group fragmentation', but a similar situation can arise when one is supposedly addressing the whole class but becomes involved in lengthy talk with pupils close by, so that the others cannot hear clearly. Rutter *et al.* (1979) point out the dangers of such actions:

> Relatively inexperienced teachers in all schools seemed to have difficulty in maintaining contact with the class as a group, and were particularly likely to concentrate on individuals, either to give specific instructions on

work or to deal with disruptive behaviour. The effect of this focus on the individual was often to lose the interest and attention of other members of the class, with adverse consequences in terms of the children's behaviour. In the schools with less satisfactory behaviour and less good examination results even the more experienced teachers tended to focus unhelpfully on the individual to the detriment of overall class management.

Kounin also drew attention to the skills of initiating and terminating an activity, and research by Partington and Hinchliffe (1979) endorses the importance of these aspects of movement management:

> Many of the observers drew attention to critical events at the beginning and end of lessons. It seemed that the successful teacher usually arrived at the classroom before his pupils, personally admitted them to the room, probably in single file, gave a friendly word here, a gentle admonition there, as his pupils passed him at the door. This was seen as establishing himself with the class, prior to a swift and compelling start to the lesson . . .
> . . . The ends of lessons did not attract as much attention as the beginnings. It seemed that badly managed classes 'disintegrated' when the bell went and pupils left without any reference to the teacher.

Rutter *et al.* also found that teachers in successful schools in their study began and ended their lessons on time. The teachers ensured organised endings perhaps by recapitulating on the main points of the lesson, reading out or commenting on some of the pupils' work or allowing silent working to continue. In each case they anticipated the end of the lesson and allowed time for packing away books and materials.

If one delays the start of a lesson to wait for latecomers to arrive this implies that one has not planned to use the full allocated time. It is inevitable that pupils will sometimes arrive late, particularly if they come from different parts of the building, but if a prompt start is not made after allowing a reasonable time for them to arrive, they are liable to drift in at their leisure. One should not interrupt the lesson to deal with latecomers but they should be seen later at a suitable time to give their explanations. The following extract is a transcript of an incident from a student's lesson, and may well be typical of the sort of unhelpful practice referred to by Rutter.

> He had been speaking for some minutes to the class of fourth year pupils when a boy entered from the back of the room and sat down.
>
> *Teacher:* What time do you call this Richard?
> *Pupil:* (*Looks carefully at his watch then back at the teacher*) Two fifty three.
> *Teacher:* Right, you're ten minutes late.
> *Pupil:* (*Studying his watch again and replying in a matter-of-fact manner*) Eight minutes, sir.
> *Teacher:* Do I get an apology?
> *Pupil:* Uh?
> *Teacher:* Do I get an apology?
> *Pupil:* (*Continuing in the same manner*) Yeah. Sorry about being late.

Teacher: Do I get an explanation?
Pupil: No.
Teacher: Why?
Pupil: Because I can't.
Teacher: Why were you late?
Pupil: I can't tell you.
Teacher: What kept you when every other person got here on time?
Pupil: No . . . No I ain't tellin' you. Sorry. (*Quietly*) This girl . . . No I ain't tellin' you . . . Sorry. (*Again his manner is not embarrassed or even apologetic.*)
Teacher: (*Continues to look at boy for about ten seconds but the boy shows studied unconcern. He turns to face the class and continues with the introduction.*)
The incident was not brought up again during or after the lesson.

Regardless of how inappropriately one feels the student managed the incident, as the pupil had entered unobtrusively, he could have been seen later when the class were working rather than interrupt the momentum of the lesson. The public examination may have contributed towards the boy's cheeky reply which challenged the student's authority.

It is very important to start the lesson with some urgency, not only to capture pupils' attention but also to create an organised and efficient atmosphere. Ideally the lesson should be introduced with an air of pleasure and expectancy, as if unwrapping an unexpected gift for the pupils, not with a sense of duty, dispensing their daily dose of medicine.

The ways in which a teacher asks questions and deals with pupils' replies can also affect the momentum of a lesson and this will be discussed later.

Smoothness

When there is a transition from one type of activity to another, it is important that this should be done smoothly. Most teachers have at some time turned away from talking to a class to play an extract from a tape, to put up a wall chart or find a passage in a book, only to find that the tape is at the wrong part, the wall chart won't stay open, they can't find the passage in the book. The pupils become restless and some begin to talk. The continuity of the lesson has been broken, and unwanted behaviour is more likely while the teacher is occupied rectifying the situation.

Kounin identified circumstances which produce *jerkiness* – a lack of a smooth transition from one type of activity to another, or breaks in the continuity of one activity. There are many occasions when the flow of an activity is broken by circumstances beyond the teacher's control. A window cleaner might appear at the window, or a pupil might interrupt a discussion with a message from the headteacher. However, the teacher can produce 'jerkiness' by poor management. Adequate preparation beforehand would ensure that the tape is at the right place, the chart stays open, and the page in the book is marked; but there are many other ways in which teachers interrupt the smoothness of class activities.

Referring back to a previous activity, then resuming the original one, Kounin describes as a *flip flop*. I have noticed when lecturing to students that if I stop what I am dealing with to mention something that I had forgotten earlier, there are noticeable signs of annoyance as they shuffle around to find the relevant notes. Kounin uses the terms *dangles*, *truncations* and *stimulus boundedness* to further distinguish the nature of the break and whether the original activity is resumed, but the important feature common to them all is that the smooth flow of class activity is interrupted.

The following extract from a lesson shows how an experienced teacher can manage to introduce appropriate blackboard work without interrupting the flow of his lesson. He is discussing architectural features of buildings and is explaining what a gargoyle is to a group of thirteen-year-olds:

> *Teacher:* You've probably seen them sticking out of the sides of old buildings and churches . . . (*turns to board and begins a rough sketch of a gargoyle but continues talking to the class*). . . . They carry the water away from the gutters . . . clear from the walls. . . . They're really ugly . . . grotesque sort of faces (*continues the sketch but looks round at one of the pupils*). Hold still a minute, Larry . . . (*pretends to use him as a model. Larry tries to suppress a smile and groans; others laugh*).

The teacher was not engaging in unnecessary talk as he drew on the board. Had he neglected to sustain contact with the group, even for that short period of time, the smoothness and progression of the lesson would have been interrupted.

Unwanted behaviour can also occur during transitions between activities which entail pupils moving to another location. Inexperienced teachers soon realise that one must give carefully worded instructions before letting pupils collect apparatus in a laboratory, say, unless the pupils have already learned to move about in a controlled and orderly way. Here, unruly behaviour is not only dangerous but also disrupts the lesson.

The following extract is from a lesson given by an experienced teacher. It is taken from the start of the lesson and lasts only about one and a half minutes, during which the teacher attempts to introduce a discussion. The introduction must stimulate some interest in the subject, but in this case it is unsuccessful. The extract illustrates some of the features that Kounin has drawn attention to, and these go some way to explain the unwanted behaviour which occurs and the lack of interest shown by the pupils. The lesson begins with a class of fourteen-year-olds seated quietly and facing the teacher:

> *Teacher:* Now, it's a short lesson so we're going to take . . . what in fact some of you wrote about yesterday . . . quite well. Something

that's been in the news a great deal lately and that is this hijacking business (*turns and writes on the board as she continues talking*) that's going on (*turns to face class*).

With a difficult class it would be unwise to turn away from them at such an early stage, before one had fully gained their attention and involvement. It certainly wasn't vital to write anything on the board yet, and on this occasion it provides the opportunity for one boy to start fiddling with an elastic band. The use of the word 'business' also suggests that the teacher is detached from the subject (see p.69).

Teacher: I looked up the meaning of the word 'hijack' . . . Put it away . . . put it away (*turns to write 'origin' on board*) and it says in the dictionary 'obscure origin' (*raising voice*) What does (*turns to class*) origin mean? . . . Origin?
Pupil: (*While the teacher is still speaking*) Where it comes from, Miss.

She has turned away again and one or two pupils begin to make audible comments. She hears this and raises her voice in response. A boy at the back rapidly calls out the answer, as the teacher immediately repeats her question. The teacher ignores this.

Pupil: Where it comes from. (*General noise as others call out answers.*)
Teacher: No, no . . . no . . . can't hear you . . . can't hear you . . . Jennifer (*looks towards girl*) . . . Origin?
Pupil: Origin means where it's come from.
Teacher: (*Looking at boy who has called out*) Origin means where it's come from.

General noise reduces but continues, and as Jennifer fails to answer promptly, a boy at the back clearly calls out above the noise and the teacher accepts his answer. Another pupil then answers but before the teacher has time to respond there follows a great deal of calling out from the rest of the class.

Noise continues in the room and is clearly unrelated to what the teacher is saying.

Teacher: Now . . . What I . . . John (*loudly*), I'm glad you know so much about this subject because you obviously know more than I do, more than the papers do, more than the Italian government does or the Chief of Police, more than the hijackers themselves it seems! (*As she turns away, John huffs on his nails as if to say 'Aren't I clever!'*).

As well as handling the question and answer session badly – refusing to accept calling out, naming pupil to respond, then accepting calling out – she has engaged in 'actone overdwelling'. The meaning of the word 'origin' is not important and detracts from the main theme getting underway. It would have been far more appropriate to read out some extracts of what the pupils had written previously 'quite well' (damning with faint praise) and hence re-focus their attention on the subject. She has also introduced a 'truncation' because she was about to define 'hijack' but went back to the word 'origin', and we hear no more about 'hijack'. She engaged in 'behaviour overdwelling' by nagging John. There had been talking in the room for some time, so she also failed to act promptly and decisively in response to unwanted behaviour. In Kounin's terms, she had failed to show 'withitness' (see p.117).

> *Teacher:* (*Leaning forward on desk so that she is speaking from a little above the height of the pupils' heads and in a rather tired voice. The expression on her face says 'It's going to be another one of those days!'*) Now in order to make sure we discuss the subject (*pauses for three seconds as the noise continues*) and not what we're going to do on Saturday morning and Friday night, we'll have a secretary as we've had before (*raises her eyes and brows and looks to the back of room for five seconds, without standing up however, in a vain attempt to check the noise*) . . . secretary we've had before (*gets quieter as she continues*) in order to get some sort of points . . . at the end of the discussion. (*Raises voice.*) Should we in fact, . . . should governments give in to the hijackers' demands?

Her own behaviour shows lack of interest in the subject, and the attempt she made to check the noise had no clarity – it did not stand out clearly as few people noticed she had stopped talking. She stopped briefly before and continued, so one can expect her to do so again. She has failed to introduce the discussion in a lively way, mainly because she has not spoken about hijacking! She also failed to exercise control over the communication in the room.

Movement management, or maintaining momentum and smoothness in a lesson, was shown by Kounin to have a far greater association with reductions in unwanted behaviour than any methods used to react to that behaviour. Putting it more simply, prevention is better than attempts to cure.

Silent working

Excessive noise often arises when a class is allowed to talk about the work they are doing. Discussing ideas or working together on a problem can be a valuable learning experience for pupils, but it has some disadvantages for the teacher and might be better left until the class can work quietly. When pupils are permitted to talk, the noise level can slowly build up in a room, and one can never be sure that the conversation is concerned with the task set, or that some pupils are not merely copying from others. From time to time it will be necessary to remind the class to work more quietly, without requiring absolute silence. In these circumstances, the teacher can be forced into giving instructions in a voice raised above the noise, telling the class to work quietly, and soon he will find himself continually checking the noise, as it quickly builds up after each reminder. It might be preferable to stop all talking after the first bout of noise, so that pupils then have to work on their own for the remainder of the lesson. In this way they might learn to exercise more care on subsequent occasions.

Although it may be unfashionable to say so, it is probably a good thing to train children to work on their own and in silence on some occasions. Kendon (1967) suggested that research into information processing supported the hypothesis that the human brain is capable of dealing with only limited amounts of information at a time. For the same reason that a speaker will look away from his listener as he organises his next utterance, it may be that in order to develop our own ability to solve problems or think creatively we need the minimum of distraction, so that we can become completely absorbed in our own thoughts. Some people prefer a background of sound such as music, but that probably does not demand their attention. Most people work better in silence on tasks requiring cognitive processes and, were this not the case, it is unlikely that libraries would have evolved as places where there is quiet and little distraction.

Observations in schools by Rutter *et al.* (1979) support this view, 'Lessons in the successful schools more frequently included periods of quiet work when the teachers expected the pupils to work in silence'. Even talking which is apparently concerned with a given problem may not necessarily be helpful in reaching a solution. Instead it may be 'an effective time-waster, providing an alternative activity to solving the task' (Bruce, 1973).

For certain tasks, then, children might be required to work in silence so that some demands are made on their own resources. In practice, though, and particularly with younger children, it is rare to see a pupil sitting quietly wrestling with a problem and really making an effort to puzzle out a solution. If the next step is not obvious or the next idea immediately forthcoming, it is all too easy for him to ask someone else or to leave it, rather than make a sustained effort to think for himself. Children must be given the experience of success through striving, as this is a major factor in deriving satisfaction from work. As Carol put it, 'You can't talk in Mr Marks' lesson, you just have to work . . . so after a while you work, and you enjoy it because you're learning a lot' (Furlong, 1976).

Questioning

A great deal of teaching involves asking pupils questions and consequently there has been considerable research into various aspects of the subject. The point has been made earlier that when teachers assume the right to question pupils and sometimes choose not to respond immediately, they claim a degree of higher status. When pupils do not answer appropriately, they challenge that claim; when they do, they validate it.

It is generally agreed that the main functions of questioning are:

to create interest and motivation;
to improve insight and understanding;
to provide diagnostic information for the teacher and pupil; and
to keep pupils alert and accountable.

The first three functions are generally prompted by thought provoking questions whereas for the last, short factual questions are more likely and there are clearly overtones of power as there is an implied responsibility on the learner to know the answer. It would be quite acceptable to use thought provoking questions with a group of university students in a seminar but they might feel affronted if asked short factual questions as there are connotations of being tested on one's knowledge.

It is immediately evident that teaching differs from other occupational and social contexts as teachers almost invariably already know the answers to the questions they ask. This can have unfortunate consequences as it may affect the manner in which the question is asked. A simple question such as 'What does that mean?' may be asked in a way which suggests one is genuinely interested in the answer. This would be conveyed not only in the vocal intonation but by an intrigued or puzzled facial expression. A listener would not only be likely to give some thought to the question and hence become more involved, but would feel that his answer would be given consideration. On the other hand, the tone of voice and manner can convey that the question is in fact a test. The teacher does not sound interested in finding out the answer but in checking whether the pupil *knows* it or in revealing his ignorance to the rest of the class. The motivation which arises in the pupil is therefore concerned with getting the *right* answer rather than in the nature of the answer itself. Another pitfall for the teacher who has become over-familiar with a particular subject is to treat pupils' answers in an automatic, matter-of-fact manner. The reply may be predictable and expected by the teacher but for the pupil it may be a new discovery or the result of some effort to attend. It is therefore important to show pleasure or surprise, or at least to nod approval so that the pupil's contribution is seen to be valued. Even if the answer is incorrect it is better not simply to dismiss it but to find some aspect which is of interest or to suggest why such an error might easily be made.

Thought provoking, or 'open' questions, as opposed to 'closed' questions which require specific answers, can certainly increase pupils' involvement and hence can be a positive feature of good classroom management. However, it may first be necessary to have cooperative and responsive attitudes before such questioning can take place. It is frequently assumed that open questions promote more responsiveness from pupils and many studies have shown such a correlation. However, Hargreaves (1984) in a series of careful observations of two classes taught by the same teacher, showed that it was the greater responsiveness of one class, in particular a small group of pupils, which probably *allowed* the teacher to ask more open questions than in the other class. It is not simply that open questions *cause* greater responsiveness, it may first be necessary to have conditions in which open questions may be asked and Hargreaves speculated on the risks involved.

> My own ethnographic observations suggest that open questions can pose management problems for the teacher, since they authorize pupils to indulge in long and sometimes irrelevant answers, which leaves the teacher with the unpleasant task of cutting off the speaker in mid-flight as well as the task of restoring relevance. Moreover, the long answer is not always audible to, or comprehensible by, other pupils, and this then requires the teacher to repeat or explain a pupil's contribution. Long pupil answers sometimes lead the rest of the class to become bored or distracted and the teacher has to develop strategies to cope with such routine troubles.

To avoid such problems it might be preferable to split up large groups for discussions though the teacher then has the problem of seeing that each group keeps to the task set. Closed questions which require short factual answers, if handled well and distributed widely among the pupils, can help maintain the momentum of a lesson. Such questions can rapidly test children on what they know and are therefore an incentive for them to attend to the teacher.

It is also important to word one's questions properly, so that they are clearly understood and do not require re-phrasing, though if a teacher has one particular answer in his mind he wants to elicit, it can sometimes be very difficult to formulate the right question. This is inflexible behaviour, however, and can lead to teachers not accepting some correct answers because they are not the particular one required, as in the following extract from a revision lesson on triangles:

Teacher: Triangles all have straight sides. Yes, now um . . . can you define them or tell me what they are in full? What sort of shapes are they? . . . What's the full description? . . . What sort of shapes? . . . Now, we've established so far that they have three straight sides, but what are they really? . . . What are they? . . . What's the real description?

Pupil: Polygons.

Teacher: Yes they are polygons but I don't want to go into that for a moment. They're special polygons and we can use a special name for them can't we, because they are . . . particular sort of polygons . . . Now I don't want to tell you what they are . . . Remember when we went . . . when . . . when we did it before . . . um . . . I pointed out to you the difference between a certain part of the triangles, and the triangle itself. . . . Well now, I'll just give you a tiny bit of help. These are triangles. Right? (*Points to five cut-out traingles on the board.*) They are bounded or sur-rounded by three straight sides. That's important. . . . They are straight sides. Not any old sides. But what are they really? John?

Pupil: Quadrilaterals.

Teacher: Oh steady now, steady . . .

The children in that lesson were surprisingly well behaved and eventually provided the required answer, which you may not have guessed was 'plane areas'. If this teacher had been faced with a difficult class, however, such repeated re-phrasing and rigid attitude towards answers would have had a disastrous effect on the pupils' attention, dramatically slowing down the momentum of the lesson. Incidentally, the amount of time spent on that one point would be regarded by Kounin as *actone overdwelling*.

The use of questions which require thought and extended contributions from pupils are very valuable in promoting conceptual development, but are perhaps better left to small group discussions or well-disciplined classes. If question-and-answer sessions are used with a new group, poorly phrased questions, rigid attitudes towards answers, or the disorganised shouting out of answers should all be avoided.

When pupils give speculative answers it may be preferable not to reveal whether they are right or wrong. Once the right answer is established, the class are no longer motivated to find out for themselves, and if incorrect answers are ruled out they can use the strategy of guessing to get the right answer by the process of elimination, but without any real understanding. I once heard a third-year boy in a small special needs group describing a car racing round a corner and he gestured with his hand to describe its movement. I could have taken this opportunity to give a short lecture on the physics of motion but instead I asked each of them what happened to the wheels when a car raced round a corner. They all agreed that two wheels would lift off but disagreed about which two these would be. They looked expectantly at me to provide the right answer but instead I acted as devil's advocate. This can encourage pupils to reflect on their understanding and become more involved in the problem. To those who thought the wheels nearer the kerb would lift I asked whether they had seen a motorcycle going round a corner. Everyone knew that it inclined towards the bend so surely a car ought to behave in a similar way with the off-side wheels lifting? This delighted those who had chosen that possibility so I asked them to imagine themselves as passengers in a car which suddenly swerved round a bend and to think which way they would be thrown. After some discussion they agreed they would be thrown away from the bend so why did this not also happen to the car and hence the near-side wheels lift? This prompted considerable argument, each side trying to account for these anomalies. Having publicly committed themselves to a particular view, they either had to change their minds or defend their positions and hence examine the problem in greater detail. In Piaget's terms, the incongruities had produced a state of disequilibrium which they needed to resolve. At the point where the teacher provides the answer the motivation ceases, and it is far more satisfying if one can find the answer for oneself, as this group did by the next session. In case some readers are unsure of the solution I shall leave it open in the hope that they experience some of the frustration which prompted the pupils to find out!

With a larger group it would have been much more difficult to get such a discussion underway and to keep everyone involved. Techniques such as redirecting a pupil's question by asking if anyone else can give an answer or checking whether everyone is following by calling on those who are not volunteering their views can be helpful but, nevertheless, the problems of quiet, reluctant or lengthy replies can still arise and the pace of the lesson will be lost.

Different subjects impose different constraints on the type of questions which can be asked (Barnes, 1969). For example, in subjects such as the sciences or English one can often ask for analysis or speculation from the pupil whereas other subjects, such as modern languages, have a very strong factual content and do not easily lend themselves to this form of question (Brown and Edmondson, 1984).

Young children are usually eager to call out answers, and questioning sessions can easily become disorganised and chaotic. To avoid this problem teachers sometimes preface their questions with a reminder about the way to behave: 'Now, hands up . . .' Having said this, it is of course essential not to accept any answer which has been called out, if they are to learn the practice.

As children get older, they should be expected to contribute in an orderly manner in large groups but without necessarily having to raise their hands. It is important that the teacher indicates unambiguously who should be talking by looking at and, perhaps naming the pupil. Instead, what frequently happens is that the teacher glances away when someone else calls out and thereby appears uncertain whether he will wait for the nominated pupil to reply, so the calling out persists. In such circumstances an experienced teacher remains looking at the pupil in question and sometimes gives a further non-verbal sign of attention such as inclining or moving towards him, while at the same time raising a hand towards the interrupter, to keep him 'on hold' until he is ready to answer him. The practice of choosing when, or if, to respond to a pupil is an expression of the teacher's authority (see p.31). If two pupils were talking and a teacher interrupted, the speaker would be unlikely to raise a hand towards him, finish the conversation and then turn to enquire what he wanted.

With large groups it is essential that pupils should contribute in an orderly way and that everyone should attend. The teacher must therefore play a central coordinating role in this process. However, if one wishes to promote pupil discussion in a small group, other strategies are called for. To discourage pupils from directing all their comments to the teacher, it is appropriate sometimes not to look at the speaker, so that he turns to look towards his peers, hence making them more likely to reply. Any signs of approval or disagreement from the teacher will continue to express the role of arbiter and will not encourage free discussion between the pupils.

As suggested earlier, questions can also be used to check that pupils understand what they are doing. I observed a group of eight-to-nine-year-olds multiply with the aid of apparatus. The problem was to multiply 34 by 6 and each child had correctly set out the problem and calculated the right answer thus:

$$
\begin{array}{r}
34 \times \\
6 \\
\hline
24 \text{ (6 sets of 4)} \\
180 \text{ (6 sets of 30)} \\
\hline
204 \\
\hline
\end{array}
$$

It therefore appeared as if they understood the process as they had meticulously used their blocks on a card divided into units, tens and hundreds. However, constructing six piles of four blocks, counting them, converting them to 'ten' blocks and so on is a lengthy process during which one can lose sight of the problem. Everyone could show me the answer but when I asked what were six sets of thirty four, or even six times thirty four, nobody could tell me. It was evident that the apparatus had been used just as mechanically and mindlessly as algorithms sometimes are. Children frequently operate mechanically with little thought for the processes which underlie their actions and appropriate questions can reveal this lack of understanding.

In summary, the use of questions which require thought and extended contributions from pupils are helpful in promoting motivation and conceptual development but may give rise to management problems in large groups. In these contexts short, closed questions can be useful in checking pupils' understanding and, if handled with pace and widely directed, can help to keep the group alert and accountable. Pupils should always be made to feel that their contributions are acceptable and, if appropriate, valuable.

The three perspectives on unwanted behaviour discussed in this section are all important for the teacher. A knowledge of the associated causes may help the teacher to understand the children, and perhaps develop a more tolerant attitude towards those who persistently misbehave. A knowledge of the possible ways in which unwanted behaviour can actually be rewarded may help the teacher to avoid promoting the very thing he is trying to stop. Finally, a knowledge of the circumstances in which the unwanted behaviour is more likely to occur, together with an understanding of group management and questioning skills, will suggest ways in which such behaviour can be prevented or at least reduced.

6 Dealing with Unwanted Behaviour

So far we have been largely concerned with creating an atmosphere in which pupils will feel inclined to work and cooperate rather than misbehave, on the principle that prevention is better than cure. Preventing unwanted behaviour requires secure, confident actions and lively sensitive teaching, and it is only within this context that pupils can be expected (or even should be expected) to behave in a disciplined way. The content of this chapter is not intended to serve as a substitute for good teaching. It does, however, acknowledge that we do not live in a perfect world, and teachers must learn to deal effectively with unwanted behaviour, particularly on the first occasion it occurs.

In the first chapter, it was suggested that when teachers successfully exercise rights which pupils do not have, they express their status and hence reinforce it. The fact that teachers can issue reprimands, punishments and rewards clearly distinguishes them from pupils, who cannot reciprocate. It follows that when a teacher successfully exercises such rights, even in relation to one pupil, he also affirms the status differences between himself and the rest of the class. However, in resorting to such powers, one runs the risk of undermining the bases upon which one's authority should rest, that is one's knowledge and effectiveness as a teacher. Pupils may then attribute their compliance to fear or reward rather than respect. This presents teachers with a dilemma and an understandable reluctance to use punishment, but if a pupil has effectively withdrawn from an authority agreement, short of persuasion, there may be no other option. It is, therefore, very important for teachers to understand the factors which influence the result of action they take to deal with unwanted behaviour. It is not the intention here necessarily to recommend or condemn any of the various ways in which teachers typically deal with unwanted behaviour, but merely to offer some insights into their use.

It is possible to adopt three courses of action in relation to an act of unwanted behaviour from a pupil. For the purpose of discussion each will be described separately, though in practice teachers often combine various treatments. First, we can attempt to follow the unwanted act by treating the pupil in ways which he finds unpleasant or aversive. The principle we rely on is that he will suppress the behaviour which brings unpleasant consequences. Second, the teacher may attempt to ignore all unwanted behaviour, so that it becomes pointless for the pupil. In conjunction with this, desirable pupil behaviour is rewarded. The principle we rely on here is that, as learning theory tells us, the desirable behaviour will increase as it gains attention, this process being aided by the fact that it serves no purpose for the pupil to misbehave. Various forms of behaviour modification can be considered within this approach. Aversive treatment and, less obviously, rewards are evidently aspects of a teacher's power in Weber's terms, as an unwilling pupil is thereby made to comply (see p.44). Third, the teacher may attempt to get the pupil to *understand* why he should not behave in certain ways. The hope is that he will subsequently choose more acceptable behaviour because he understands and accepts the reasons the teacher has given. Persuasion has a certain ethical appeal, in that it seems to rely upon the pupil exercising self-control in the absence of either punishments or rewards.

A moment's reflection will reveal that aspects of all three approaches are often combined. The miscreant is publicly harangued, while being given reasons for the reprimand. A punishment follows, but the teacher also seeks opportunities to offer praise for any effort. However, the possible results of any one of these treatments are subject to so many variables that it is preferable to consider them separately.

Aversive treatment

Teachers usually have a range of unpleasant things which they are empowered to do to pupils in an attempt to change their behaviour.

Use of fear

If people fear they will come to some physical harm they are likely to modify their behaviour to avoid such consequences and many teachers have used the strategy of 'using one's temper' (rather than 'losing' one's temper) to intimidate pupils and hence gain their compliance. However, this is very unwise as any physical assault on pupils is now illegal and such threats are therefore meaningless. During a dispute, teachers should be particularly careful to avoid any physical force, including touching pupils, to emphasise an instruction as it is likely to be interpreted as aggressive. The pupil may retaliate and later give a very distorted account of one's actions. There is a very narrow line between a serious, firm and assertive manner and an aggressive threat and it is essential to communicate the former unambiguously as pupils will sometimes consider it advantageous to misinterpret one's behaviour. Actual physical punishment, even when it was legal, always had its limitations, as regular offenders realised it really did not hurt that much and could be used as an easy mark of toughness with those who believed it did.

There are, of course, more subtle ways in which fear is used to promote desirable behaviour. As Ausubel (1968) noted, 'The motivating force of an examination lies more in the fear of failure than in the hope of success.' Fear of failure can be highly motivating but, as Ausubel pointed out, this must be distinguished from failure itself, which can decrease motivation. By using such pressures to persuade children to study, we therefore tread a narrow path, and it seems inevitable that some pupils will fall by the wayside. Fear of failure may produce effort, but some success must be guaranteed.

Use of guilt and embarrassment

Feelings of guilt are unpleasant and teachers sometimes attempt to make pupils feel ashamed or embarrassed about their actions. Social disapproval can be a powerful means of changing people's behaviour, and statements ranging from mild admonishment of the type 'George ... don't do that' to the more direct rhetorical questions 'Aren't you ashamed of yourself?' or 'Do you behave like that at home?', all serve to bring this form of pressure to bear. Systems of order marks, being 'on report' or having one's name and offence read out in assembly, all rely to a certain extent on bringing some shame or embarrassment on the pupil. The old-fashioned Dunce's Cap now seems a cruel application of this principle, particularly as the unfortunate pupil was made to feel ashamed because his *work* was not good enough: many slow learners must have suffered considerably under such treatment. The danger now is that some children may qualify as slow learners simply because no such demands or pressures have been put on them.

Another variation in this form of social pressure is the threatened 'withdrawal of love'. This can only be used where there is an existing good relationship between the teacher and pupil, and where the suggestion of disapproval therefore has implications for that relationship. Such disapproval from the teacher is usually non-verbal and covert. This affirms to the pupil the special relationship which exists, as it does not expose him publicly. The glance says 'I don't expect that sort of thing from you, John' and guilt gets to work.

Ausubel suggests that this type of effect is the result of the pupil's 'need for affiliation', 'I'll do this because I want you to like me'. He goes on to point out that this 'need' may not always operate in the teacher's favour. The adolescent who associates with anti-school groups may disrupt lessons in order to consolidate his position among his peers (see p.84).

Use of nuisance or frustration

Teachers are able to limit pupils' freedom and impose irksome tasks.

This category of unpleasant treatment would include the use of detentions, clearing up, and giving extra work of one form or another. The nature of the activity which the pupil is expected to carry out is usually boring, such as writing 'lines', and he is therefore deprived of using his time as he chooses and forced to engage in an essentially non-rewarding activity. There has been much discussion as to whether such meaningless tasks as 'lines' should be given. However, the effect of the approach does rely upon the fact that the task is a nuisance to the child. Indeed, it is sometimes argued that 'meaningful' activities, such as essay writing or mathematical calculations, are only devalued in the pupil's estimation if they are set as punishments. Conversely, if there is any satisfaction or enjoyment to be gained, then the activity might not serve to deter future misbehaviour. It might therefore be better to reserve extra work within school subjects for those occasions when it is intended to improve a pupil's progress or understanding, rather than to serve as a punishment for misbehaviour.

Depriving pupils of privileges or activities that they enjoy is a treatment similar to imposing irksome tasks, because it also relies on making them feel frustrated.

It is possible, as a last resort, to suspend a pupil from school and what pressure this brings to bear may vary, though he is likely to miss the companionship of friends. The parents or guardians will be made aware of the seriousness of the situation, if they did not already know, and may experience some difficulties in managing the child at home. The most obvious outcome would presumably be the removal of a disruptive influence from the school.

Clearly, for pupils who may already be disaffected with school, teachers have very limited power to force them to comply and the use of such power is likely to worsen relationships and increase disaffection (see p.34). As Tattum (1982) concluded from his study of disruptive pupils, their behaviour was determined by whether they liked and respected the teacher and not on what consequence could be brought to bear on their actions. It is important to bear this in mind in the subsequent discussions of the effective use of aversive treatment and of rewards.

Giving reprimands

It is sometimes necessary to discourage pupils from a particular course of action because it violates the interests of the school, other pupils or themselves. This can be done in the form of a non-verbal, verbal or written message that the teacher is not pleased with the behaviour, and it can be sufficient to remind pupils of their responsibilities and the authority agreement is thereby preserved. Kounin called such attempts to correct pupils' behaviour *desist techniques*, but his research failed to identify any variables which had a significant effect in determining their success. He therefore conluded, 'The techniques of dealing with misbehaviour, as such, are not significant determinants of how well or poorly children behave in classrooms'. On the other hand, it would be true to say that teachers who have established well-ordered classrooms use desist techniques effectively, though they are seldom needed. It is probably in the first meetings that pupils either learn to respond to or to ignore the teacher, and the manner in which desist techniques are administered then, may affect classroom management. Their successful use later, however, is possible only in the context of responsive and cooperative behaviour to which they, in turn, contribute. If an unruly atmosphere has developed, desist techniques will have little or no effect in improving the situation, and their frequent use is only a consequence of the pupils' disregard for them.

It is therefore useful to consider the manner in which reprimands and warnings are given so that they can be administered to the best effect and do not adversely affect relationships. The principles which apply to addressing the class (see p.55) are also relevant here. Before giving a reprimand to a large group it is essential to gain attention and silence with an appropriate contact signal, and an atmosphere of seriousness can then be created by speaking in measured tones, without bodily movement. This can be enhanced by using the middle or lower registers of one's voice, as this gives an impression of self-control whereas a high pitched outburst suggest the reverse.

Mitigation

French and Peskett (1986) found that teachers of infants differed in the way they gave 'pedagogic instructions' from 'control instructions'. The distinction was one of immediate function as they acknowledged that any instruction seeks to exert some control over pupils. Pedagogic instructions were concerned with the accomplishment of learning tasks and were delivered in straightforward imperative structures, for example. 'Press the little button now', or 'Put them in one by one'. On the other hand, control instructions were marked by a variety of features which attenuated or mitigated the potential impact of the direct imperatives. The simplest of these was the use of 'please' or an added endearment term, for example, 'Peter, stop the talking please' or 'David, sit down love'. Mitigation also occurred in the vocal quality of the control instruction which was sometimes delivered in a friendly or 'jokey' tone. The addition of positive evaluation such as '. . . there's a good boy' or a reason, for example, 'Don't do that now otherwise others won't be able to hear', also served to mitigate the impact. French and Peskett suggest that 'because teachers generally do not use unmitigated control instructions, they are able to hold this option in reserve for occasions when firmness is required'. Following an unheeded mitigated instruction the teacher can use a direct imperative, which is presumably intended as a reprimand.

Another way of interpreting mitigated instructions is that they are an attempt to retain the authority agreement as the teacher avoids the implications of power in the direct imperative by giving an additional message about the friendly and cooperative nature of the relationship. Mitigation is unnecessary with pedagogic instructions as the basis upon which authority is being claimed is clearly the teacher's knowledge of the subject, which is not in question. Similar ways of making 'directives' appear less obvious have been discussed by Holmes (1983) and it is not surprising to find mitigation occurring with older children, particularly in informal classrooms, though the form it takes varies. One would almost certainly hear vocal mitigation, the use of 'please' and what French and Pleskett described as 'request formats' and 'minimisation of adjustments', for example, 'Could you just . . .' Control instructions need not have overtones of coercion if delivered quietly and inconspicuously which may be why they were found to be more effective than loud reprimands (O'Leary *et al.*, 1970). Reprimanding in general terms to a whole class would also mitigate the impact for the particular culprits as it would publicly protect their identity and imply that others might be capable of similar infractions. A glance at the offenders would be all that was necessary to show that one was not acting thus out of ignorance.

The dilemma faced by teachers is to try to retain an authority relationship, based on cooperation, without jeopardising any firmness with which they may subsequently have to act. Mitigation must take place with complete integrity or it is likely to be interpreted as weakness by the pupils, who would then be more inclined to resist attempts to force them to comply. An approach which could be helpful in some situations is to write to the pupil about the problem in question.[1] For example, in the incident over litter (p.88), instead of forcing the boy to comply I could have simply picked up the paper myself but subsequently written to the pupil along the following lines:

> Dear Darren,
>
> This morning at break when I was on playground duty I asked you to pick up some litter and you refused. I had seen you drop it but didn't want to make a fuss over such a small thing. You may have just been having a joke but I thought your behaviour was rude and unnecessary.
>
> Please help to keep the school tidy by putting litter in the bins.

How does one close such a note? 'Yours sincerely' seems too formal and I would be inclined simply to sign my full name. A christian name alone would appear ingratiating unless that was how the teacher was normally

---

[1] I am grateful to Professor Andy Hanson of Chico State University California for this suggestion.

addressed. The relationship presented by taking the initiative to pick up the paper and then sending a private note, is one which does not acknowledge any threat to one's status and maintains respect for the pupil by mitigating the reprimand.

This approach would lose its credibility if used too frequently, but it has the advantage over a private interview in that the pupil does not have to take any further action. In a face to face talk the pupil might feel that the teacher's motive was to extract an apology which, in fact, would probably be the only satisfactory outcome. With a private note, the pupil may subsequently choose to take the initiative and apologise and thereby gain in self-respect.

Holmes (1983) pointed out that 'Teachers may avoid ostentatious demonstrations of authority by using less explicit directive forms, but children soon learn from experience that the teacher's every wish is their command'. In relation to pupils' behaviour, therefore, teachers' hints, suggestions, requests and commands are all part of the same continuum as there is an underlying understanding that pupils are expected to comply. However, the milder forms give pupils the opportunity to cooperate willingly and hence the teacher may avoid emphasising the power difference which is expressed by giving commands. They also leave a teacher the option of not insisting that the pupil complies, whereas when a direct imperative has been used, particularly if accompanied by other displays of dominance, this would be seen as backing down.

Reprimanding effectively

When it has become necessary explicitly to exert control over a group, one's behaviour must not express any doubts either about the unacceptability of the pupils' conduct or one's right and ability to correct it.

As a general rule it is better to say and do as little as possible as it is far better to leave pupils to infer what they are doing wrong and how they can rectify the situation. I saw a good example of this while watching a group of ten-year-olds taken by an experienced teacher. One boy threw his rubber to a friend and it fell on the floor. As the latter was about to get it, the teacher merely said 'Leave it' and looked at the boy who had thrown it. Rather shamefaced, he went and picked up the rubber and gave it to his friend.

When it is necessary to say something, it is important to think of the actual words one intends to use, because in the heat of the moment it is easy to blurt out the start of a sentence which is impossible to complete sensibly. Perhaps there is a small disturbance in the room as the teacher enters. Appropriate cliches come to mind, such as 'If you think you can behave like that then you're very much mistaken', or 'I don't expect to leave the room for five minutes and find you fooling around when I come back.' What might emerge if the teacher is not careful could be something like this: 'If you expect . . . to behave like that when I come into the room . . . then . . .' The first few words make it difficult to complete the sentence constructively, and the impact of the reprimand is lost as the teacher stumbles on in an incoherent way. Even if the sentence is completed, it can often be very tortuous – I heard one teacher say: 'Come on . . . this is not going to be . . . enough cooperation from you!'

Even if one is very articulate it can be a mistake to deliver lengthy reprimands, particularly if they contain an instruction to the class, as the following example from a lesson transcribed from video-tape illustrates:

> The teacher enters the room together with a class of fourteen-year-old pupils. There is considerable noise and movement in the room and the teacher waits at the front, facing the class, for fifteen seconds before saying: 'All settled where you're going to be? (*1 sec.*) Right, now you can all jolly well go outside and come back into those places as if you were . . . (*2½ secs*) . . . er (*1 sec.*) . . .' (*continues to speak for 4 secs, but this cannot be understood from the tape partly because of the noise of the pupils going out but also because she spoke more quietly.*) Immediately the instruction to go outside had been given, some pupils started to move and, while the teacher tried to think of a suitable description, the majority of the class were moving out and the noise was considerable.

The teacher failed to achieve sufficient contact before the lengthy message and also did not control the pupils' movements adequately. If one fails to anticipate premature movement, as in the example, then the first pupil to show any intention of leaving his desk should be stopped abruptly. By moving away while the teacher is still talking, pupils reduce the effect of any reprimand and convey a lack of respect, so instructions must be carefully phrased.

A short reprimand, when the class is silent, is usually quite sufficient to stop unwanted behaviour, but it is tempting to try to 'ram home' the message by saying more. Criticism or justification for one's actions often gives the impression of nagging, and it is far better to discuss the matter with the class or individual later, if necessary. In the example above it might have been better simply to have settled the class and begun the lesson, but having decided to send the pupils out the teacher need only have instructed them to stand up, and when there was complete silence said, 'You came in *very* noisily . . . Now you will *quietly* . . . go and line up outside the room. Girls.' (Indicate to move). Increased volume and appropriate pauses while the teacher scans the faces of the pupils provide all the emphasis needed. At the end of the lesson one could remind them of the need to enter classrooms in an orderly manner, and perhaps warn them of the consequences that will follow if they do the same thing again on the next occasion. It would still be a mistake to dwell too long on such a minor matter, however.

A long diatribe in response to unwanted behaviour is rarely necessary and will have the opposite effect to the one intended if the pupils feel it is unfair. It is hard to understand what Mr Baker felt he was achieving by the following harangue delivered to a class of thirteen-year-olds (Wragg and Wood, 1984a).

> 'Are you eating? Well stop moving your jaws. Sit still. Some of you should be in strait-jackets. If you don't work then you'll have to copy out of the book. You are going to conform to my standards which are not in any way abnormal. In this life there are some people who want to work, there will be six million unemployed in the 1980s – none of you has convinced me that you are in any way employable. I'm in charge here. I can enforce it and I will. It's as simple as that (bangs fist on table). Sooner or later someone will get physically hurt. Don't push me too far. We're all human, boys and girls alike. You are my family. It's my legal right to punish you. Don't forget that.'

Such an exaggerated proclamation of one's power only suggests insecurity and at best the pupils would have been bored or amused by the outburst. At worst they would have felt angry and insulted. It is also a clear example of what Kounin termed behaviour overdwelling (p.95) and would only serve to interrupt the momentum of the lesson.

Torode (1976) considered that the actual language used by the teachers he observed was of paramount importance.

> Mr Howie's problems were not, in my estimation, a consequence of his non-verbal communication patterns, his pose, dress or tone of voice. In all these respects he performed precisely the character of the normal teacher if . . . there is such a thing. The incessant and sometimes violent conflict which characterised his lessons was directly attributable to the teacher's failure to give an enduring definition of the situation while that situation was being enacted.

Giving 'an enduring definition' refers to the ability to present statements of 'external rules' which the teacher enforces in an impersonal but inevitable way. Torode contrasts Mr Howie with his more successful colleague:

> Mr Crammond told them: 'Right now. I think we know the order of events. You've got to get on by yourselves today, and I don't want to see anybody off their seats.' Here the familiar definition is reasserted. The inner picture, the definite *we* is posed as knowing 'the order of events' watched over in the outer picture by the less certain *I*. On the other hand the *you* is portrayed as quite dominated by external necessity. 'You've got to . . . .' The *I* appears again later in the utterance, again in an indefinite outer picture contemplating a definite factual state of affairs.

This detailed analysis, though interesting, over-emphasises the function of language at the expense of other factors in the situation and would certainly not be relevant to those occasions when non-verbal behaviour alone is used very effectively. The particular language used is only part of the way in which a teacher attempts to give an enduring definition to the situation. Though it can be one factor in conveying impersonal and uncompromising attitudes, it is important to remember that the meaning which is conveyed by any interpersonal communication depends upon the *total* behaviour, so that two teachers could use identical words but achieve entirely different effects (Wragg and Wood, 1984a). It is also crucial that pupils learn that threats will be backed up by action, and in the previous example it is significant that one boy who did leave his seat was immediately 'belted' by Mr Crammond.

Failure to back up threats would eventually result in the pupils' ignoring them. Any intermittent and therefore unpredictable punishments would be regarded as unfair by the pupils because other similar misbehaviour has passed unheeded. Pupils should quickly learn that one's threats are, in fact, promises.

It is also a mistake to notice or comment on unwanted behaviour without doing anything about it. For example, a teacher might mention that a pupil is not in his correct seat, or that he has not done his homework. If no further action is taken to put the matter right, given that there is no adequate excuse, this creates the impression either that the offence is trivial and probably permissible, or that the teacher is powerless to do anything about it. Unless one is prepared to go to the trouble of seeing that the offence is corrected, it is better not to notice, though this does have implications for the teacher's 'withitness', which will be discussed later. In the following extract from Torode's paper we see Mr Howie making this mistake:

Teacher: Right, would you turn to page fourteen *please!*
Cannon: (*Shouts*) Where's Barrie?
Teacher: Right, would you all stop talking, please? Cannon sit down (*no change in overall level of noise*). Now, just before we went away . . .
Various
Boys: (*Interrupting*) Are we going away?
Teacher: (*Continues, ignoring interruption*) We were talking about sets.
Boys: Sex! Sex!
Teacher: (*Interrupts uproar*) Scott, why is your book not covered? And Davis, yours as well.
Davis: I just got it.
Teacher: You didn't just get it today. The next thing I want to talk about is the interaction of sets.
Cannon: What was that word you used?

Though this extract contains a number of other mistakes, it was clearly unwise to comment on the uncovered books without seeing that something was done about them. (It also illustrates the pupils attempting to take control of the communication by interrupting and questioning, and the teacher talking above noise in the room. It is almost certain that Mr Howie's non-verbal and vocal behaviour would have been consistent with the 'loser' image suggested in the transcript.) Also, if one persists with mitigated forms of instruction when they are no longer heeded it can sound like pleading for cooperation and one frequently hears students imploring 'Will you *please* stop the talking!', or making ambiguous statements such as 'There's too much noise in here' which does not specify exactly what is required.

Wood and Schwartz (1977) suggest that *clear directives* – unambiguous instructions stated in an uncompromising way – are the most effective means that parents can use to ensure that children do as they are told, and the same principle may apply in school. One's determination will be expressed more in one's voice, facial expression and gaze than in what one says and any teacher who finds difficulty in conveying such attitudes may not actually be feeling them strongly.

There are clearly a number of points at which a teacher might intervene with a reprimand, though the formal punishment, such as detention, may come much later. These would include the moment the child was about to misbehave and any time during or after the misbehaviour. The majority of research suggests that if a teacher intervenes as a child is about to, or just beginning to, misbehave, a repetition of the misbehaviour is less likely than if the child had been allowed to complete the act. There are several possible explanations why early intervention should be more effective, apart from the fact that a child 'caught in the act' is less likely to deny his action. The teacher clearly demonstrates that he is alert, so that the child may feel more liable to detection. The act of interrupting the behaviour is itself a statement of the teacher's control and status in the situation. (In contrast, a child interrupting a teacher might be reminded that such behaviour is inappropriate.) The child may also be denied any reinforcement which would have resulted from completing the act, such as making a friend laugh or engaging others in some disturbance. Early intervention also prevents the spread or escalation of unwanted behaviour, so that the teacher has only to deal with a relatively minor offence. A more esoteric explanation is that the fear of detection becomes associated with the initial action or thought of action, rather than its completion. Gnagey (1975) expresses this view very clearly, 'Teachers who can see deviances developing should stop them before they get started. Otherwise, the fear operates only after the fact.'

There are, then, many good reasons why unwanted behaviour should be nipped in the bud, though this is sometimes easier said than done. Nevertheless, there may be some circumstances when a teacher is able to allow a child to make mistakes and learn from them. The question of mitigation also arises in that it may sometimes be better for the long-term relationship not to intervene immediately in a public situation but to have a quiet, private word with the pupil later.

Withitness

The term *withitness* was coined by Kounin to describe the ability of a teacher to communicate to children 'by her actual behaviour (rather than by simple verbal announcing: "I know what's going on") that she knows what the children are doing, or has the proverbial "eyes in the back of her head".'

The concept is concerned with the teacher being able to select the pupil who is instigating the deviant behaviour (in Kounin's terms, the *target of the desist*) at an early stage before he has had a chance to involve others. If the teacher selects the wrong pupil – makes a *target* mistake, such as punishing an innocent child – or reprimands for a minor offence while more serious ones are occurring (Mr Howie did just this when he noticed the uncovered books yet allowed the noise and interruptions), he will fail to communicate 'withitness'. He might also make a *timing* mistake so that the unwanted behaviour had spread to others or increased in seriousness before he intervened.

This is a useful concept because if the teacher shows 'withitness' this will help to reinforce other impressions of being in control. It was narrowly defined by Kounin for the purposes of his research, but one could extend the principle to incorporate other aspects of teachers' behaviour.

The ability to name children in the class in the early meetings will also suggest an alert awareness, for example. The reverse is very evident when the teacher gives the wrong name, particularly when reprimanding: the impact is totally lost, as the pupils are able to correct the teacher and regain some initiative in the communication. Naming one pupil often has more effect than a general reprimand directed at the whole class. Apart from conveying 'withitness', it might also highlight the vulnerability of every individual, whereas a reprimand to the class sustains each pupil's anonymity, though this may be what one intends (see p.112).

Remembering to carry through any sanctions one had promised also contributes to an impression of being in control or 'withit'. Having instructed a pupil to remain at the end of a lesson, or promised to deprive a class of a favourite activity, it is vital to remember. Otherwise one gives the impression of being muddle-headed, and pupils will soon learn to ignore one's threats and instructions. Other aspects of good organisation, such as being in the right place at the right time with the required books and equipment, or anticipating changes in arrangements, such as dental inspections or sports practices, all help to convey the impression of efficiency and 'withitness'.

Factors affecting punishment

As we have seen, punishments in schools are not particularly aversive and it is unlikely that any pupil who is really determined to challenge the teacher's authority will be discouraged by them. Similarly, any teachers who fail to back up their claims to authority with efficient teaching will find punishments inadequate to force most pupils to comply. The frequent use of punishments by a teacher is, therefore, usually not a means of sustaining an orderly atmosphere but a symptom of a disorderly classroom in which the teacher is making futile attempts to force pupils to comply. In cooperative teacher-pupil relationships the authority agreement usually prevails and coercive power is seldom required. Unfortunately, there are occasions when pupils act irresponsibly and unless checked may learn that they can exercise considerable control over what happens, or fails to happen, in the classroom. This is not helpful to anyone and the dedication in *Beyond Control?* (Francis, 1975) expresses this succinctly:

> To 3B4/5
> with whom
> and therefore for whom,
> I could do nothing.

It is important that punishment should be used in a beneficial way for all concerned and a more detailed examination of the variables involved is necessary to explain why they may be more effective for some teachers than others.

Negative reinforcement

An important distinction should be made between aversive treatment used to suppress a response, which can be regarded as punishment, and aversive treatment used to increase the probability of a response, which can be regarded as 'negative reinforcement'. A rat might receive a shock every time it tried to feed from a specific container and so would learn to avoid food in that container. The feeding response would have been suppressed by punishment. In contrast, a rat might be trained to jump on a ledge to avoid receiving or to terminate a shock. The shock would therefore have been used to train a specific response and so can be regarded as a reinforcer of the response.

It is helpful for teachers to think of this distinction in the way they administer aversive treatment to pupils. Rather than declare 'The next person who talks will finish this work during the lunch hour', it would be better to say 'Anyone who has not finished this work by the end of the lesson will do so during the lunch hour'. In the former statement the response, talking, is being suppressed by the threat of punishment, whereas in the latter, the desired behaviour, working, is being reinforced. Having once promised to punish talking, the teacher may be forced into penalising a well-behaved child who perhaps only offered a friend some quiet advice, or who may have been answering a neighbour whom the teacher did not hear. Punishment suppresses one response but does not necessarily offer an alternative, so that a child may sit quietly but still not be working. If the teacher later leaves the room, punishment for talking becomes less likely, so noise begins again. Where working is being reinforced the pupils may not wish to risk losing some of their lunch hour by wasting time. In general it is preferable to use aversive treatment in such a way that the pupil *can avoid or terminate it by appropriate behaviour*, though there may be instances where this is not possible. One must also be sure that the pupil is able to do the work set, and hence avoid the adverse consequences, otherwise he might learn to avoid the task altogether by truanting, rather than attempt to overcome his difficulties. Allowing pupils to avoid punishment by 'illegal' means, such as failing to attend detentions or hand in the extra work, will by the same principle reinforce those avoidance behaviours.

Severity

The fact that punishments can differ in severity raises important questions for the teacher. Do the more serious offences merit harsher consequences – should 'the punishment fit the crime'? Should a teacher deal more leniently with the first occasion on which a pupil commits an offence, and more harshly with the continual offender? Such questions are not confined to schools, and the debate on the treatment of criminals demonstrates that there are no simple answers.

The conclusions to be drawn from research into the effects on children's behaviour of the intensity of punishment are complicated by several factors. Understandably, it has not been possible, for ethical reasons, to administer severe or painful punishments. Experimenters have, therefore, compared the effects of treatments such as mild and severe disapproval, or relied upon the sound of a loud noise as a punishment. It is also not surprising that the effect of severe punishment differs according to whether or not children are told which behaviour is prohibited and given reasons why they should not do certain things. More seriously, experimental studies seldom take into consideration the motive for deviant behaviour or the nature of the behaviour itself. As has already been seen, the reasons why children misbehave are varied and complicated, and children may well choose certain behaviour simply because it is forbidden. Not all children are motivated to misbehave to the same extent, but experimental studies may fail to take this into account, and sometimes a random sample may simply be punished for an arbitrary response such as playing with an attractive toy, without being given any reason for such treatment. One must therefore be cautious in generalising the results of such research to the treatment of unwanted behaviour in the classroom.

As suggested earlier, relatively severe levels of punishment can induce fear or anxiety, and Aronfreed and Lapp (Aronfreed, 1968) demonstrated that this could be unhelpful in certain circumstances. When young children found a discrimination task difficult, their performance was hindered by harsh punishments given for wrong choices. It is surely common sense that if a child does not know what to do, or how something is to be done, then severe punishment for mistakes will only make matters worse.

Some support for the notion of a 'short, sharp shock' comes from Gnagey (1975): 'Researchers have found that a quick, firm rebuke is much more effective than a low-keyed punishment that has to be repeated on increasingly severe levels. This does not call for inquisition techniques for every minor infraction, but it does call for reprimands which pack a wallop.'

It certainly seems sensible not to train a child to develop a tolerance of punishment by subjecting him to treatment which varies little in intensity from what he has previously experienced. One must nevertheless still take into account the seriousness of the offence in choosing an appropriate punishment, as Biehler (1978) points out: 'In the early days of Merrie England all offences – from picking pockets to murder – were punishable by death. The petty thief quickly became a murderer; it was a lot easier (and less risky) to pick the pocket of a dead man and, since the punishment was the same, eminently more sensible. The laws were eventually changed to make punishment appropriate to the degree of the offence.'

Though experimental findings tend to support the popular view that more severe punishments have greater inhibiting power, this relationship is seldom clear in practice (Rutter *et al.*, 1979). Given the type of punishments available in schools and the other variables in the classroom which will be discussed later, it is unlikely that more severe treatment will necessarily have greater success in changing pupils' behaviour in the desired direction. It might do just the opposite. If the punishment for a particular misdemeanour is not regarded as 'fair' by the majority of pupils, the teacher will have in effect abused the authority agreement.

Consistency

Associated with the idea of 'withitness' is the notion of consistency, because it requires the teacher to be alert to unwanted behaviour when it occurs. A consistent approach is usually taken to mean that every offence is dealt with, but one could of course be consistent in failing to give punishments – by deliberately ignoring unwanted behaviour, for example.

A consistent or reliable approach to punishment is important, particularly during the initial meetings with a group, because it helps to establish the rules which the teacher feels are important. Every time a rule is broken without penalty it becomes more difficult subsequently to enforce that rule. There are a number of reasons for this. A teacher may be regarded as inadequate if he fails to notice offenders, or as 'soft' if he obviously notices but takes no action. Any reinforcement which arises from a 'successful' misbehaviour will therefore tend to make it more likely to happen again. Another disadvantage of inconsistent punishment is that it will be regarded as unfair by the unfortunate child who receives it, because others have previously escaped unscathed.

If consistent application of punishment is desirable, then it follows that all offences should be detected and receive appropriate treatment. There is no better argument for keeping rules to an absolute minimum, unless one wants to spend the major part of one's time enforcing them. Once rules have been established and the pupils are behaving in a cooperative way, then one may wish to temper justice with mercy by overlooking some transgressions. However, a teacher who starts by making rules and then fails to enforce them is, in effect, training the children to flout his authority.

Personalisation

Two aspects of punishment have been distinguished by Ausubel (1968). One is the 'non-reward' or aversive treatment as a consequence of misbehaviour, the other is 'the penalty for moral infraction which takes the form of blame, rebuke, reproof, chastisement, censure or reprimand'. This latter aspect can be thought of as 'personalising' the punishment. Hargreaves (1975) makes a similar distinction between 'deviant acts' and 'deviant persons'. A teacher might therefore administer a punishment in a way that suggests it is the normal consequence of a deviant act, or could, in addition, chastise the offender. For instance, a child who had been warned that if he wasted time he would have to complete his work during the lunch hour, could be dealt with in either way. A totally impersonal approach would involve the teacher calmly and privately saying 'I said that if you wasted any more time you would have to do this work during the lunch hour. Come to my room at twelve o'clock and finish it then.' With a personalised approach the teacher would appear much more emotionally involved with what the pupil had done, and might deliver the same punishment in a threatening and public manner: 'Trust you to waste your time! You have to be different from the others, don't you? Well, I warned you! Come to my room at twelve o'clock sharp and bring your work – what there is of it!'

The first treatment merely punishes the act but does not attach any blame to the offender. The message conveyed is that the pupil has chosen not to work at that time and so must make it up later, whereas in the second case there is an additional message that the offender is inherently wicked, which accounts for his behaviour. There are dangers in adopting this type of approach, apart from the obvious one that the pupil may begin to view himself as irredeemably bad and behave accordingly. In Chapter 5 it was suggested that some unwanted behaviour may be aimed at creating excitement or annoying the teacher, and in such cases an emotional outburst would be likely to aggravate rather than improve the situation. If an aggressive reprimand is given publicly the pupil may not cooperate, or may give an insolent reply so as not to lose face in front of his friends. A minor offence can escalate out of all proportion in this way, and the pupil who successfully provokes a teacher may gain in prestige. Also, when a teacher shows any sign of aggression towards a pupil it is essential that it is effective, because the child who does not comply forces the teacher into more extreme action.

For unwanted behaviour which has no malicious intent, for instance when it is due to carelessness or thoughtlessness, it may not be significant whether or not the child is subjected to some verbal reproof. There is even some evidence to suggest that blame may subsequently assist children to be more critical of their own actions (Aronfreed *et al.*, 1963). On such occasions, however, a teacher does not usually wish to chastise, whereas when confronted with a pupil who is continually disrupting the work of the class, a calm intervention might seem beyond the capacities of a saint. Nevertheless, personalised verbal aggression brings only short-term relief and merely establishes a pattern for future interactions. In order to minimise the dangers of an escalating conflict, of labelling the child as 'deviant' and of becoming the victim of malicious teasing, it is probably safer to give punishment in a way which conveys to the pupil that he is having to face up to the consequence of his action, but that you don't hate him for his behaviour.

Relationships

The variables which have been discussed so far have been concerned with administering punishment itself, but the outcome will also be affected by the characteristics of the child receiving the punishment. Factors such as age, sex, temperament, experience and any motive prompting the behaviour could all be significant in explaining the ways individuals vary in their reactions to the same treatment. To complicate the matter further, the type of relationship which exists between the teacher and pupil may also affect the result, and it is reasonable to expect that the relationship will in turn be affected by the punishment. If a child dislikes a teacher, he may regard any punishment as unfair treatment and evidence that the teacher bears a grudge against him. Not only will there be no desirable effect on the child's behaviour, but the relationship could be worsened. In the reverse situation, Wright (1973) reached the following conclusion: 'There seems little doubt that both at a relatively superficial level and also in a more committed and long-lasting sense when the child likes the punishing agent the probability that punishment for misbehaviour will result in later self-control is much increased'.

It does not follow that punishments should be given only to those with whom good relationships exist, as this would be neither practical nor sensible. It does, however, strengthen the case made earlier that one should not show dislike or anger when punishing a pupil. It also suggests why teachers who have good relationships with a class are often very reluctant to use punishments and give the pupils every opportunity to comply voluntarily within the authority agreement.

Offering an alternative

An important question for teachers is whether or not a child who is misbehaving could achieve the desired result by behaving in other, more acceptable ways. Solomon (1964) pointed out that punishment can be very effective in helping children control impulses, provided they have an alternative way of getting what they want. A rat which receives a shock when choosing one pathway will readily travel another route if it is available. Puppies learn not to urinate in the house not only because they are punished for doing so, but also because an alternative site is provided. In the same way a young child will learn that some activities, such as kicking a ball, are more appropriate outdoors. If, however, one chose simply to ignore the inappropriate behaviour and reward the desired behaviour (an approach which will be discussed in the next section) training would be a lengthier process. Of course, it is not always possible to be sure exactly what children hope to achieve by behaving in unacceptable ways, but teachers might try to allow children legitimate means of securing some of their more probable objectives (see p.82) For instance, Mr Cramond (in Torode, 1976) allowed a five-minute break at the end of each lesson during which pupils were permitted to talk among themselves. It is, then, more likely that they would have controlled impulses to talk at other times, particularly as they also ran the risk of losing the privilege. This practice would also offer some reward to pupils who are keen to avoid work. The opportunity to engage in a preferred activity, even if it is only talking or gazing out of the window, seems a sensible incentive to offer pupils, provided it is dependent upon their working satisfactorily for the rest of the time.

On the assumption that some pupils misbehave to seek attention from teachers, they should receive it at times when they are behaving appropriately. This may sound obvious, but it is very common for teachers to regard such moments as relief from torment and they therefore tend to ignore the children.

Some pupils seem intent upon challenging the teacher's authority, and it may well be that the school does not offer legitimate ways in which all pupils can be given responsibilities and share in the decisions which affect their lives. If pupils have played a part in formulating the rules which govern their behaviour, they will be less likely to challenge the teacher's right to enforce those rules.

Inevitably certain aspects of school will seem boring to some pupils in contrast to their lives outside. In extreme cases they may be expected to work from the same books, sit at the same desks and listen to the same voice for long periods in the day. This is clearly undesirable, and might well prompt some pupils to seek to relieve the boredom. The greater variety a teacher can introduce, the less need children will feel to create their own excitement. Some subjects, such as drama and games, as well as extra-curricular activities, allow pupils to engage in exciting experiences, but all teachers should be searching for opportunities to enliven their lessons. Within a context where pupils are able to obtain such objectives by acceptable means, they will be less likely to resort to measures which could result in punishment. However, one must accept that some pupils may have objectives which the school cannot sanction.

There are certainly other factors affecting the short- and long-term effects of punishment. For example, Gnagey (1960) showed that the status of the pupil receiving a reprimand could affect the attitude of the rest of the class towards the teacher: if a 'leader' responded compliantly to a reprimand this enhanced the teacher's reputation as a good disciplinarian, whereas a 'low prestige' boy responding in the same way did not influence other pupils' opinions. Once again, the danger of open confrontation in a class was highlighted by the fact that if a 'leader' responded defiantly to a reprimand, the class subsequently regarded the teacher as a poor disciplinarian.

It is, then, hardly surprising that the results of punishments are frequently unpredictable and considerable skill is required in applying them effectively. Unfortunately some children are regularly subjected to punishment because they continue to misbehave. This is not only undesirable but also demonstrates that it can cease to have any beneficial effect. For these reasons other methods of dealing with unwanted behaviour can be advocated.

Positive approaches

More positive approaches relying on praise, reward and persuasion are considered as an alternative to using aversive treatment. As with resorting to coercive power, their use may imply that the authority agreement is in question. In some cases, such as using rewards, the teacher is clearly relying on measures which are unrelated to the knowledge and skill upon which the authority agreement is mainly based.

Ignoring unwanted behaviour

Instead of subjecting the child to unpleasant treatment, an alternative approach is to reward desirable behaviour and ignore behaviour one wishes to eliminate or 'extinguish', to use the Behaviourists' term. Behaviour modification, aspects of which have been discussed in previous chapters, represents the most systematic application of this method which derives from the work of Skinner (1971). In general, the method provides a suitable context for unwanted behaviour to be ignored, but it can also include aversive consequences such as punishments or 'negative reinforcers'.

The basic principles are quite straightforward; any actions which are rewarded will tend to be repeated and learned, whereas actions which have no consequences for the individual will not continue. Though unpleasant consequences will suppress an action, they will not necessarily extinguish it, that is, it may reappear if the consequence is altered. Behaviour modification has many advocates because it has been shown to be effective in helping to overcome a wide range of human problems, and so it merits serious consideration from all teachers. It offers an alternative to the traditional use of punishment, though in many respects there is nothing new in its method. Rewards, in the form of praise from the teacher, stars, house points and privileges have long been a feature of school life, and the notion of 'sweetening the pill' must be a fairly universal standby when children are reluctant to obey. Usually, however, rewards are used in conjunction with punishments, rather than ignoring undesirable behaviour – which can be difficult with large groups of children.

Teachers acquire the habit of looking out for undesirable behaviour, and to show no reaction, not even a pained glance or a 'give me strength' appeal to the heavens, can be difficult to learn. as mentioned on page 84, other children will provide the attention that the teacher denies, and sometimes the behaviour is so disruptive or dangerous that it cannot be overlooked. When unwanted behaviour is first ignored one can anticipate that it will initially escalate. The danger is, then, that the teacher who has been suppressing his natural irritation will decide 'Right, that does it!' and let all hell break loose. Long before this breaking point is reached a time-out procedure, whereby a child is quietly removed from the room, is recommended (see p.87). A Department of Education and Science report, *Truancy and Behavioural Problems in some Urban Schools* (1978), suggests that shared teaching can fulfil a similar function, without actually having to remove the child from the room:

> In an area where physical violence is never far away, the teachers argue that new methods of working, especially team teaching, have virtually eliminated classroom disruption. Where one teacher has difficulty, it is easy to send the pupil concerned to work with another teacher without any sense of failure or embarrassment.

Even so, one wonders whether getting a difficult child to move from his seat is ever easy, and the manner in which he is approached seems crucial if a confrontation is to be avoided. It is difficult to maintain that one has ignored unwanted behaviour with such procedures, and the critical element in the effectiveness of the whole approach seems to be the teacher's ability to control his reaction and apparently remain calm. Before one can expect to control others, one must be able to control oneself.

Praise and rewards

If unwanted behaviour is being ignored, then it is essential that the desired alternative behaviour is made as attractive as possible, and so lessons must be interesting and varied. Even then, for some children this may prove insufficient to gain their involvement. Some teachers are against using any reward other than praise, as they feel that children will learn to view work only as a means of ensuring personal gain, rather than being worthwhile for its own sake (Lepper, Greene and Nisbett, 1973) The use of reprimands and punishments has been considered as a form of coercive power and a similar danger exists with giving praise and rewards which can be regarded as 'reward power' and may therefore detract from the teacher's authority. If a child will not make any effort, however, he may be persuaded to work for an appropriate extrinsic reward until such time as he becomes sufficiently involved to find the work itself interesing.

Many suitable rewards are readily available in schools; Hamblin (1971) lists twenty-eight items used by one teacher, including ten minutes' free time for studying, reading or playing educational games, listening to a record, sweeping the floor, and exchanging tokens for pencils, exercise books and other school supplies which the child would normally have been given. One teacher I worked with allowed the children to bring small toys which they no longer wanted so that others could purchase them with tokens in the 'swap shop'. In some cases it may be possible to arrange with parents that certain home privileges, such as watching television or going out, will depend upon school behaviour during the day. Less obviously, the personal attractiveness of some teachers is likely to have reward value for the pupils and is therefore a source of power in schools as it can be in other interpersonal relationships.

Many of the variables discussed in the administration of punishment are also significant in the effectiveness of rewards. In relation to the size of the reward itself, the general principle that large rewards induce greater efforts is complicated by a number of factors. One pupil may work hard in the hope of praise from a teacher, whereas another might attach no value to it whatsoever. One can also become bored with the same rewards day after day, so fresh incentives to effort are required. Rewards, therefore, have no absolute value but are measurable only in relation to the extent that they increase the probability of a response. (A similar operational definition can be used for punishment, in that its intensity is related to the extent that it decreases the probability of a response.) Wherever possible, a choice of rewards should be offered to children so that they can find something for which they would like to work. An alternative is to award tokens which can later be exchanged for a reward.

The timing of rewards is also important. Although immediate praise or reward might be preferable in some respects, it is not sensible to interrupt behaviour one is attempting to promote. It is also considered more mature to be able to work for long-term rewards, rather than only for those which bring immediate gratification. A baby cannot understand that it must sometimes wait when it wants something, but an adult should.

Consistent or continuous reward, that is the practice of rewarding every instance of desirable behaviour, is helpful in establishing the behaviour rapidly, but there is also a danger that it will disappear even more rapidly if the rewards are withdrawn. In practice, it is extremely difficult to note every instance of the target behaviour unless one is working with a very small group, and in any case an inordinate amount of time spent on praise or rewards could detract from the point of a lesson and slow down the pace. If rewards are given intermittently then the desired behaviour is more likely to continue when they are withdrawn.

It is not necessary here to go into further detail regarding all the variables associated with administering rewards, but it can be seen that they need to be appropriate to the child, frequently varied, and given more often to young children or to those who are just beginning a skill and experiencing slow progress. When one also considers that children may be receiving rewards for differing improvements in work or conduct, it is not surprising that token economies and other forms of behaviour modification are seldom used systematically in normal class-rooms, as large groups make their implementation very cumbersome. Nevertheless, when teachers are given regular and continuous help at workshop sessions in applying the techniques, considerable success has been reported with a variety of educational and behavioural problems (Harrop, 1974; Cook, 1975; Presland, 1978). Behaviour modification is more often used where children have special problems, such as low ability or behaviour disorders, and are working in small groups, usually in a special school or unit. The problem then arises of how to maintain the desired behaviour when the child is returned to a normal school where the system of rewards, together with the practice of ignoring misbehaviour, is absent. If a child has been taught a skill such as reading, one would not expect this to be lost, but he could revert to old patterns of behaviour. This would depend largely on whether the conditions which supported his original misbehaviour, such as peer group attention or inappropriate teacher reaction, still persisted.

It is much more difficult to find things which children will work for as they grow older. Age is obviously an important variable in the effective-ness of a particular reward, and even social praise has to be modified. In an attempt to overcome the problem of maintaining improvements in behaviour, some Local Education Authorities have set up 'support teams' of teachers and psychologists to help the class teacher cope with children with behaviour difficulties rather than remove them to special units. One account describes the application of behaviour modification techniques to individual children in primary classrooms, for example allowing them to score goals for a favourite football team displayed on a chart, if they behaved appropriately. On some occasions the support teacher taught the class, allowing the class teacher to work on an individual basis with the pupil presenting problems and hence to build a better relationship (Coulby and Harper, 1985).

In the same way that one should punish an act rather than a person it is important to direct one's attention and praise to what pupils have done or achieved rather than to the pupils themselves. Direct praise expresses the power of the teacher to make pupils comply. Publicly commenting that they are 'good', 'clever', 'sensible' or whatever, implies that they have performed satisfactorily for the teacher and appears increasingly condescending as they get older. On the other hand, responding with enjoyment or surprise to a good answer or discussing and admiring a good piece of work enhances the status of the pupil in relation to the teacher and he may thereby gain a sense of pride in his achievements. Wheldall *et al.* (1986) showed that 'teacher touch' when accompanied by praise, could be an effective reinforcer of work and behaviour in four classes of five- to-six-year-old infants. The status implications of touch have already been discussed, but in this case it was clearly shown to intensify the effects of normal praise from teachers. However, if one wishes to enhance the status of pupils as they grow older it might sometimes be more appropriate *not* to touch them when praising because the tendency could be to focus the praise on the pupil rather than the work. By refraining from touching one would also avoid appearing patronising and would show respect towards the pupil. In the same way that we attempt to mitigate reprimands and punishments, it is probably better to mitigate the implications of 'reward power' when praising and rewarding older pupils.

Contracts with pupils

As it is often difficult to find appropriate rewards for older pupils, it may be possible to reach an agreement between teacher and pupil whereby both benefit in some way. Agreements, or contracts, must be negotiated willingly by both parties concerned and each should have something to gain from the arrangements. The pupil can offer better cooperation in the form of working harder or improving his behaviour, but the teacher's contribution is less obvious. There may be some lessons that the pupil particularly likes, or would like to miss, or special privileges available in the school such as lunchtime clubs or outside visits. One can then discuss an arrangement whereby the pupil makes certain concessions in return for a reciprocal concession from the school. The following account illustrates this approach and some of the difficulties involved:

Jane was in her second year of an upper school when the headteacher referred her to me for disruptive behaviour. In discussing the circumstances with the staff, it emerged that only a few were actually allowing her to attend their lessons and she was on the point of being suspended from school. She had caused a rumpus in the library and thrown a transistor radio across the room, had stuck chewing gum into a boy's hair and committed other similar disruptive acts. She was frequently late for lessons, and when questioned by the teacher would often get abusive and storm out of the room, sometimes locking herself in the toilet. The surprising thing was that she seemed to want to remain at the school. She was very seldom absent and, when sent home for misbehaviour, would return to wait for her friends at the gate. We therefore made an agreement with her. She would lose one point each time she was late for a lesson, did not bring the proper equipment, or disrupted the lesson. She could gain a point by working well during a lesson. The concession from the school was that she would not be suspended unless her weekly total of points lost exceeded ten. They were also conceding, therefore, that she could continue with her misbehaviour provided she was able to earn enough points by working to stay within the ten points limit.

It was more difficult to get the staff to accept this arrangement than the pupil. The headteacher did not want to enter into any 'bargains' with a pupil although, by previously allowing her to miss some lessons, concessions had already been made. A few staff already coped well and did not want to bother with the arrangement. Once the scheme was underway some teachers tried to deduct points as a punishment for any offence; for instance when she was rude to a member of staff in the corridor, two points were deducted. These had to be returned as no agreement had been made in this respect. They also wanted to take off points in a punitive manner – 'Late again! That's another point you've lost! – when in fact it was essential to behave in a non-provocative manner. If Jane argued that it was not her fault that she was late and so shouldn't lose a point she was quickly informed that she was disrupting the lesson and would lose a further point if she continued. In this way staff were relieved of the considerable anxiety of how to avoid a hostile confrontation with Jane, without appearing to let her do as she pleased. They were able to respond in a calm, non-aggressive manner so that the whole character of the interactions altered. For several weeks Jane kept just within the limit by working hard to make up any necessary points on the final day and thereby avoid suspension. Then a surprising thing happened. She stopped going out with a boy who was also at the school, and this coincided with a change in her behaviour. Why this should have happened is difficult to imagine, but she began to behave in a much more acceptable way, sometimes ending the week with a positive total of points. This marked a turning point for her, as, although she never became a model pupil, she was able to be contained within the school without the help of a contract in subsequent years.

One can argue that the contract alone did not bring about the change in Jane's behaviour. The arrangement involved her receiving daily individual attention from a sympathetic teacher to discuss her progress, and this may have had a beneficial effect. One could equally argue that such attention would perpetuate the bad conduct, because it would inevitably be discontinued once she had improved. The contract obviously had no direct effects on any personal problems she had which may have predisposed her towards such behaviour. The most noticeable change which resulted from the arrangement, however, was in the nature of the interactions between Jane and certain members of staff. The contract enabled the staff to remain calm and non-provocative in response to her behaviour, as well as requiring them to reward her efforts. She was therefore not able, or did not feel the need, to escalate the situation in the way she had done previously.

If one has a particularly disruptive pupil there is no harm in discussing what he values, or would like changed, in the school. It might be possible to reach some agreement whereby both parties have something to gain, and future interactions could be much more benign as a result.

The notion of a contract may also be useful in making older pupils aware of their own responsibility for creating a context in which learning can take place. In cases where a teacher has lost all control in a class it might be possible to offer to make the lessons more interesting in return for their cooperation and attention. The content and proposed method could be discussed beforehand so that the class become more actively involved in the process. This would probably only be appropriate with older secondary pupils as such negotiation after 'defeat' would acknowledge that the teacher had lost authority and had no power to retrieve the situation. It might also require the services of a neutral support teacher to mediate and monitor the agreement to see that both sides honoured the contract, though there would still be no guarantee that the pupils would cooperate even if the teaching improved.

Pupils train teachers

In the previous example, in order to change Jane's behaviour, the teachers had first to change their own. This principle has been demonstrated in reverse by Graubard and Rosenberg (reported by Gray, 1974) who taught problem children how to make their teachers behave better towards them! As one might expect, the researchers found that pupils who were frequently in trouble often complained that teachers were unfairly picking on them. Sure enough, when careful records of interactions were kept by the pupils and trained observers, a high level of negative comment from the teachers was found, although on many occasions the pupils failed to recognise the teachers' positive behaviour or misinterpreted it as hostile. Unbeknown to the teachers, the researchers selected seven children, aged between twelve and fifteen, from a class considered 'incorrigible', and instructed them in ways in which they could make the teachers treat them more positively and, using videotapes, taught them to make more accurate judgments of the teachers' behaviour.

Jess, one of the seven selected, was a particularly violent fourteen-year-old, who had apparently knocked other pupils unconscious with chairs and beer bottles and had been suspended for forty days for hitting a principal with a stick. He and the other six were trained to ask teachers for help, and then reward them with a smile and remarks such as 'You really help me learn when you're nice to me', and, if the teacher offered any words of encouragement, 'It makes me feel good when you praise me.' The smiles proved something of a problem for Jess. What actually emerged was a menacing leer, but with video-tape sessions he was taught to give a charming grin. Another technique in which the pupils were instructed was the 'Ah-hah reaction'. If the pupil felt he had understood a teacher's explanation, he would say that he did not understand. When the teacher got half way through the second personal explanation, he would exclaim 'Ah-hah! Now I understand! I could never get that before!' This technique was aimed at giving the teacher a feeling of accomplishment and making him like the pupil.

The research demonstrated that during each of the five weeks of the project the teachers became more positive towards the pupils concerned. It is interesting that later, when the teachers were told about the experiment, many of them felt it was the pupils who had changed, rather than themselves. Just as Jane's teachers had first to alter their behaviour to bring about a change in interactions, so Jess and the others had to alter their behaviour for the teacher to relate differently to them.

Pupils control themselves

The approaches discussed so far have involved one person trying to bring about changes in another, but in self-modification one person must take on both roles. There must be a strong desire to change one's behaviour if this method is to be successful, as any rewards or punishments will be self-administered. Those who have a specific goal to aim for, such as passing an examination or losing weight, are ideal candidates, as the benefits of exercising self-control will be evident. There can also be indirect pressures to keep the person from 'cheating' with the programme. He may have to discuss his progress with an adviser, who would remind him of the need to be strict with himself and help in setting realistic goals.

A student who was having difficulty in studying for an examination would first identify what he regarded as rewards. These could range from having a cup of coffee to going out with friends. Each reward would then have to be earned by doing a predetermined amount of work and, if this was not accomplished, he would have to deprive himself of the reward. Clearly for this to be successful considerable will-power or, more accurately, 'won't power' is required. It is all too easy to slip back into the self-delusion that one will feel more like working after a cup of coffee, bath or other relaxation. If someone else can be persuaded to dispense the rewards, this can be helpful, as there is less opportunity to cheat, but then the system resembles a school environment, where the teacher assumes responsibility for the pupil's progress and is in charge of rewards and punishments.

Most people need a good reason for exercising self-discipline, because it entails sacrificing short-term benefits in the hope of long-term rewards. A heavy smoker might be persuaded to give up cigarettes after a heart attack as his survival is threatened, but the 'death' that follows school failure is less certain and always more prolonged. We must not underestimate the role of examinations in providing the motivation for pupils to develop good study habits and self-discipline, but unfortunately such a system depends upon the fact that only some pupils can succeed. Perhaps the new General Certificate of Secondary Education which is designed to examine a much wider range of abilities and involves the assessment of work submitted during the course, may help pupils to exercise self-discipline.

An unusual approach to helping pupils exercise self-control requires them merely to keep records of their own behaviour. This method has been shown to be effective for teenage pupils both in America (Broden *et al.*, 1971) and in an ordinary school in England (McNamara and Heard, 1976). One method of recording required each pupil to keep a tally of every occasion that he behaved inappropriately, and another required pupils to record whether they were studying or not, whenever they thought about it. The latter method would not, therefore, give a reliable measure of the actual number of inappropriate acts, because some might pass unrecorded by the pupil. Teachers and outside observers were used to confirm that pupils' recordings were truthful and accurate.

Both methods resulted in considerable improvements in behaviour for most of the pupils participating, but McNamara and Heard found that recording every instance of inappropriate behaviour produced a superior rate of inprovement. Unfortunately, the numbers involved in the studies were small (in Broden *et al.* only two took part), so it is difficult to draw reliable conclusions, but this is obviously an approach which merits further investigation. The sheer simplicity of the scheme would make it easy to introduce with a few pupils in a school without impinging on the work of the others.

One can only speculate as to why the pupils' behaviour should have improved when they were asked to record it. The results could be explained as a form of the Hawthorne effect (the suggestion that merely showing an interest in the subjects of an experiment, making them feel special and listening to their views, may influence their behaviour in the desired direction), but McNamara and Heard offered another possible interpretation:

> At the commonsense level, making the pupil record his own behaviour may encourage him to be aware of what he is doing. Such a strategy is probably very effective with the inconsequential, non-reflective pupil who 'acts first and thinks afterwards' – the child who is not maliciously disruptive but who none the less disrupts the class because he lacks the ability to organise himself and his work.

The very act of recording probably interrupts the inappropriate behaviour which would subsequently have to be resumed, and this pause would give an opportunity for the reflection that the authors suggest takes place. (There are also similarities with the practice of confessing one's sins.) However, if self-recording became common practice in schools, familiarity might breed contempt. It would be so easy for the pupils to falsify their recording, as two girls did in the McNamara and Heard study. The authors warn, therefore, that 'while self-recording is no panacea for secondary school problems, it might well be an additional and useful strategy in the teacher's repertoire of techniques for coping with some problem behaviour of some pupils'.

The main objective in dealing with unwanted behaviour is to encourage the pupil to behave or work appropriately in the future and, in the absence of someone in authority, to exercise self-control. Cheyne and Walters (1970) point out that self-control may be mediated emotionally, because the pupil fears the consequences of being caught, or cognitively, in that the child understands that his actions are not compatible with a rule which he accepts. Emotional control would, therefore, seem to derive from aversive treatments, resulting from the teacher's use of power, whereas cognitive control is dependent upon a reasoned appraisal of the situation and is more consistent with an authority agreement. One must also consider the role of habit training in promoting self-control, as it may be that some pupils behave appropriately simply because they have learned to.

However, if teachers merely wait for children to understand and accept that they should behave appropriately then they may be waiting a very long time. One uncooperative child can ruin a lesson for the whole class and it is therefore expedient to use interim measures to persuade him to cooperate. Perhaps punishments and rewards should be seen in this context: as a means of exercising emotional control over behaviour until the child's capacity to respond to reason develops.

Reasoning with pupils

As an alternative to using coercion or reward power, the teacher may attempt to persuade pupils to comply with the demands made on them by offering appropriate reasons, as in the following conversation between a teacher and pupil.

Yes? What do you want, Brian?

Miss Evans said I got to see you.

What's the matter?

Well . . . She said I was talking, an' I wasn't.

She sent you here for talking?

Well. . . . She started gettin' on at me, an' shoutin' . . . so I swore at her.

Is that why she sent you?

Yeah. . . . But I wasn't talkin'.

Do you think it would be all right for teachers to swear at pupils? . . . If they were angry?

. . . (*Shrugs shoulders*) I dunno.

. . . You say you weren't talking when she spoke to you. Had you been warned earlier in the lesson about talking?

Yeah.

But this time you weren't talking?

No.

Were you working?

. . . No.

What were you doing?

. . . I was laughing at something.

You weren't getting on with your work?

No. . . . I done some of them, but I didn't understand how to do the others. . . . (*pause 5 secs*).

. . . If you were trying to do a job – say you had your motor bike stripped down and a little kid kept interrupting you and throwing your tools around – how would you feel?

Get angry wiv 'im I suppose.

And if he swore at you?

(*No reply.*)

Knowing you, Brian, I expect you'd politely ask him to leave . . . (*Brian sniggers*) . . . You were stopping Miss Evans doing her job – to see that you learn something – do you think it was right to swear at her?

. . . No.

What are you going to do about it?

. . . Apologise.

And?

Dunno.

Well, I'd like you to make an effort with your Maths so at the end of each day you bring me your book and show me what you've done . . . I'll ask Miss Evans to let me know how you're getting along. . . . We'll see how it goes for a fortnight. . . . Now you go and apologise to Miss Evans and tell her what we've arranged. . . . I'll expect you tomorrow at 3.45 with your work.

Sir (*Goes to leave*).

Brian . . . Who were you sitting next to?

Fred.

Don't. . . . Give yourself a chance.

Reasoning includes describing the consequences that the pupil's behaviour may have for others and explanations why specific demands are made of him. It seems only common sense to give reasons to justify or explain decisions and rules. If pupils understand why certain demands are being made, then they are more likely to make those demands of themselves.

Unfortunately, understanding the reasons does not guarantee compliance with the rules. Most persistent offenders can give all the reasons why they should not misbehave, as they have heard them many times before. One can only assume that their actions are thoughtless, ungoverned by reason, or that they have other, stronger, reasons for behaving as they do. If a pupil feels bored because he takes no interest in a subject, he may fool around, because this is much easier than making the effort to participate in the lesson. The fact that he is wasting other people's time as well as his own does not enter into his decision. He is bored and seeks an easy outlet. It seems superfluous on these occasions for the teacher to provide reasons for reprimanding the pupil, as they are probably obvious to all concerned. Some teachers are too easily trapped into the 'reasons game' by pupils whose objective is to argue their way out of trouble if given the opportunity. This exercise can waste a good deal of time and slow down the pace of a lesson as the following extract shows. The teacher is collecting essays from fourteen-year-old pupils which should have been done during the half-term break from which they have just returned:

That's the third essay you haven't given in! (*Turns to the next pupil*)
Where's yours?
My what?
Essay.
What essay? (*Teacher does not reply but stares at pupil*) I wasn't here. . . .
What essay? . . . I . . .
(*Teacher interrupts*) The one on the fly. You were here, you haven't been away.
Well, why should I spend my holidays doing homework? I've got other things to do like . . . I don't want to sit in all holiday doing homework.
So you think you're going to get your exam without doing any work? (*Pupil looks at teacher and raises head and eyebrows as if he hasn't heard*)
(*Teacher repeats*) Are you going to get your exam without doing any work? (*Pupil then looks down at a friend who joins in*) Yeah, but look, Miss. Supposing, right? We haven't done about the fly, right? And you haven't taught us about the fly, right? How can we . . .
(*Teacher interrupts*) I told you to use the library. You can't expect to be spoon-fed the whole time. Anyway I'm going to do the fly later on.
But if we went into the exam, like, we couldn't go into the library then, could we? While we're sitting there in the exam they wouldn't . . .
(*Teacher interrupts*) That's very silly. You . . . just because I give you something that isn't in a text it doesn't mean that you can't go to the library and get the information yourself. Other people have managed to.
(*First pupil again*) Miss! The fly hasn't got nothing to do with human biology though, has it?
So disease hasn't got anything to do with human biology?

Yeah, but that's not the fly.
Well, the fly has got to do with disease because it carries disease.
Er . . . Well, it's not in here is it? (*pointing to the textbook*) Anyway, I wasn't here.

It is interesting how the teacher is forced to justify her actions throughout the interaction. From the outset it is evident that the pupil is not being cooperative but makes the teacher respond to his questions (see p.31). When he is unable to make a suitable reply to the teacher's point about working to pass the exam, he makes the teacher repeat the question to gain time. He is still unable to counter this point, but is rescued by a friend who raises another objection. The teacher deals with this argument, so the first pupil raises a further objection concerned with the relevance of the topic. This is explained, so the pupil returns to the original excuse.

There is a place for such discussions because teachers should be able to justify their actions to pupils, but it was inappropriate and misleading to do so here. One could argue that the teacher presented a model of reasonable behaviour to the class, but in fact the episode served only to waste time. The issue was fairly clear: the pupil had not done the work set. If it was important, then it would still have to be done, regardless of whether he was previously absent or not. Reasons are not necessarily excuses, but they can be taken into account in considering any punishment for the offence.

It seems from the teacher's first statement that it was not unusual for homework to be disregarded. One could take the view that pupils must learn to take responsibility for their own private study, and that homework is therefore desirable but not compulsory. There is, though, a risk that if one presents homework to children on the lines of 'further suggested reading', the impression can be given that one does not really care whether or not the pupils make progress or do justice to the subject. What is worse is to present it as compulsory and then fail to enforce it, as this gives the impression of being weak and lacking in control.

It is helpful if pupils have the opportunity to express their views and even share in the process of making rules in the school. Nevertheless, there is a time and place for such discussions. The pace of a lesson can be slowed down by spending time on disciplinary matters (see p.95) and so these are best dealt with privately unless they concern the whole class. What might seem to be 'giving reasons' from the teacher's point of view can end up sounding like nagging if the pupils have heard it all before and if it is said in a whining, 'When will you ever learn?' manner. Glasser (1969) suggested setting aside special time for discussion, so that the whole class can participate in solving individual and group problems.

It is easy to be wise after the event but a more satisfactory way of handling the above interaction would be along the following lines.

Where's yours?
My what?

Have you done the essay on the fly which I set for homework?
I wasn't here.
See me at twelve o'clock and we'll arrange when you can do it. In the
meantime I'll check when you were absent (*notes pupil's name*).
But, Miss, I . . .
(*Interrupts*) Explain when I see you at 12 o'clock. We have to start the
lesson now.

The point has already been made that reprimands should be brief
(p.14), and one way to ensure this is to avoid a lengthy justification of
one's actions.

Handling disputes and confrontations

In spite of teachers' best efforts occasions will still arise when they
become involved in disputes with pupils. These often develop from a
minor offence and progress quickly to a major confrontation, during
which there may even be a physical assault. The original cause for the
intervention is quickly forgotten as the teacher's authority is challenged,
he resorts to threats, the pupil resists and is rude. By this time both
teacher and pupil are well up the 'escalation-detonation staircase' as
described by Laslett and Smith (1984). Frequently a punishment is
given not for the original offence, but for the pupil's reaction to the
teacher.

Pik (1981) suggested four 'rules' which can provide useful guidelines
for handling such situations. His first rule is that the teacher should
'Decide first whether it is worth risking a confrontation over a particular
incident. Has there been a breach of school rules or principles,
important enough to warrant intervention at that moment or would a
quiet word with the pupil later on perhaps be a better course to follow?'

In the incident concerning litter (p.88) it was clearly not important
enough to warrant the events that followed. It was as much my own
insecurity, as the pupil's challenge, which led to the escalation. When
the pupil denied dropping the paper, instead of immediately ordering
him to pick it up, a more experienced teacher might have said, 'Well, I
could have been mistaken. Could you pick it up anyway please and put it
in the bin?' This would not necessarily ensure that he did, but by
mitigating the instruction, the teacher would not have escalated the
conflict and would have been in a position to fulfil Pik's second rule,
'Leave yourself and the pupil a gracious way out'. The gracious way out
for the pupil would be to do the favour that has been politely requested.
For the teacher, it could be to pick up the litter himself if the pupil still
refused as he has not yet staked his authority on the pupil's compliance.
A letter of mild censure from the teacher could then follow (see p.112).

It might be possible to offer a compromise to the pupil so that he feels
he is being treated with consideration. Often he will be glad of any way
to release himself from the confrontation without losing face. In this

respect it is vital to avoid an audience as neither party will want to back down in public. If the teacher senses determined resistance it is better to drop the matter and see the pupil privately later. One should always try to ascertain the facts of the matter before giving a punishment as if pupils feel they are being treated unfairly they are more likely to resist. This should not necessarily be done at the time of the dispute as the teacher's priority is to maintain the momentum of a lesson for the class and to avoid a public spectacle.

The third rule states, 'Remember that threats by a teacher to use physical force will nearly always escalate a conflict very quickly and dramatically and will greatly increase the probability of the pupil reacting violently.' One does not have to use verbal threats of physical force. Aggression is largely conveyed non-verbally by moving closer, staring and appearing tense and menacing. Violent outbursts of 'temper' usually occur as a means to delay actual physical violence in the hope that the display will serve to achieve one's end but in either case there is no gracious way out for either party. Physical force from a teacher is permissible only to prevent danger to persons or property, including themselves, so it is extremely unwise to behave threateningly unless one is certain that the pupil is in no position to offer any significant physical resistance. Young children, for example, would probably comply when faced with such treatment as the difference in physical power would be indisputable. It is far better that the teacher should not show any signs of tension, even if there is obvious reluctance or aggression from the pupils. Neill (1988) offers strong support for this view from his review of research into animal conflicts. He points out that if one opponent is much stronger than the other, even a slight threat will be enough to drive the weaker opponent away. He argues, therefore, that '. . . a teacher who fiercely threatens her pupils is signalling that they represent opponents whose abilities are matched to hers.' In other words the teacher would be defining the pupil's behaviour as a real challenge to her authority. Neill goes on to argue that because threats imply preparedness actually to attack the opponent, the teacher risks manoeuvring herself into a position she cannot sustain in the face of continued resistance from the pupil. She cannot legally use violence and has no harsh punishments to back up her threats, and therefore is relying on an element of bluff. As pupils grow older it is not surprising that they therefore view such treatment from teachers as challenging and provocative: even when they do submit to the bluff they are likely to feel hostile and resentful and an emotional confrontation is the more likely outcome.

When control instructions, reprimands and punishments are delivered in a relaxed high status manner without a display of personal dominance, the pupil is more likely to accept them as a legitimate expression of the teacher's authority. If, one implies 'you know that you should do this' or 'you know these are the fair consequences of your actions' the power being claimed is presented as part of one's responsibility as a teacher in the school rather than as an attempt to intimidate the pupil. Of course, the pupil must perceive the teacher's actions as 'fair', both in the right to intervene in such ways as normal practice in the school and in acknowledging his own guilt, as it is only in his *voluntary* compliance that the expression of the teacher's power is legitimised within the authority agreement. On the other hand, when we resort to forceful dominant behaviour, implying 'you know I can *make* you do this' or 'this is to punish you', any obedience which follows can only be presented as a submission to our personal power rather than as a voluntary act. Not only is the pupil unable to present his compliance as cooperative, but also the teacher cannot then offer a compromise without appearing to have backed down in the face of the pupil's resistance.

It is extremely unusual for confrontations to arise between pupils and teachers who share good friendly relationships. When a teacher has to intervene in such cases it is probable that the liking and respect for the pupil will be expressed in his attitude and the reverse is also likely – if a teacher dislikes a pupil it will be evident in his manner. If one anticipates a dispute, therefore, it would be better first to remind oneself to show respect, concern and even liking for the pupil or at least to remain calm and polite. It is then difficult for pupils to become aggressive and they are more likely to calm down themselves. If one does show anger it should be as an expression of one's concern for the pupil and not as an attempt to intimidate him.

Pik's final rule concerns the restitution of normal relationships after the event. 'A reasonable time after a confrontation the teacher involved should take the opportunity to talk privately with the pupil before they are next scheduled to come into contact with one another in the classroom.' This does not necessarily mean that there should be a post-mortem and it may be far more appropriate to behave as if the incident had been forgotten. For example, Wragg and Wood (1984b) observed that after Mr Abel, a well-liked and respected teacher, had reprimanded two girls he apparently deliberately went over and spoke to them in a very friendly manner about their experiment. Similarly, when I had to reprimand a pupil during a lesson, I would subsequently ask a small favour of him (if the opportunity presented itself), such as to borrow a rubber or ask him to deliver a message. One tends to ask favours from one's friends and such actions were attempts to restate the cooperative nature of our relationship. There is a danger, however, that the teacher can appear ingratiating and apologetic as if he fears that the pupil will no longer like him or realises that his treatment has been too harsh. One's object should be simply to resume normal relationships as soon as the dispute is over. Clearly, the more emotional the confrontation, the more difficult this will be.

Some teachers have the gift of being able to diffuse tense situations by using humour. In one case I heard of, a young female teacher in a school for children with behaviour disorders walked into her class of fourteen-year-olds to find one tall well-built boy brandishing an iron bar in a threatening way at those around him. The atmosphere was extremely tense, but as she walked in she gave him little more than a cursory glance and walked unconcerned to her desk. 'Right,' she said, 'Pokers away, pay attention.' For humour to be effective, the teacher must genuinely see the funny side of the situation and not appear to belittle the pupils who are likely to be very sensitive at such times. In this respect it is probably vital that a good relationship already exists so that one's remarks will not be misinterpreted. If the teacher is disliked, his attempts at humour will probably be treated derisively or he will not be regarded as taking the problem seriously. Attempts to contrive humour into a situation can also easily misfire and one is then faced with coping with one's own feelings of rejection. It is all too easy in these instances to become aggressive to avoid looking stupid. On the other hand, genuine humour and relaxed behaviour can keep incidents in proportion and also help to unite the participants.

The following extract is transcribed from a video-tape and begins at the start of a lesson with a dispute between fourth year girls over seating in a laboratory. Debbie is standing and arguing with two girls who are already seated as the teacher intervenes.

Debbie:	I can sit here can't I? (*Turns and looks at teacher*) She can copy it out.
Girl on front bench:	No we haven't got a book.
Teacher: ⎱	(*Quietly*) Sit (*Pointing to bench behind*) . . . Debbie.
Debbie: ⎰	(*Talking to girl on front bench and ignoring teacher.*) Yeah . . . Well if you got a book . . . I could sit there.
Teacher:	(*Handing Debbie a book from the front bench and speaking in a quiet reasonable manner*) I'm surprised at you . . . Go on (*pointing to another seat. There is a pause of 3 seconds during which Debbie tilts her head to the side in a conciliatory manner.*)
Debbie:	(*In a softer, more reasonable tone*) Carol can sit there.
Teacher:	(*Sharply*) Look you're doing different work to everybody else.
Debbie:	(*Returning to a more aggressive manner*) I don't want to sit there on me own with them.
Teacher:	(*Loudly and firmly*) Sit there! (*Debbie moves*). (*Turns to the two girls on the front bench and speaking in a firm tone*) Right, there's your book, there's your book, get on with it.
Debbie:	(*As teacher moves away Debbie goes back to original place and snatches up a book from the bench*) I ain't finished . . . I've got this. (*Takes the book and throws it down on the bench behind, pulls her chair out in a noisy way and sits down.*)
Teacher:	You're a nasty rude girl. (*Class laughs.*)

The teacher managed to get Debbie seated elsewhere but it was clear that she would be unlikely to cooperate much during the lesson. If relationships are not to be worsened by such disputes the teacher should try to ensure that the outcome is 'better for both' (Kilburn, 1978). In the above extract, when the teacher spoke quietly to Debbie and implied that her behaviour was uncharacteristic, (I'm surprised at you), she became conciliatory in her manner. Had the teacher continued talking quietly and sympathetically instead of immediately snapping back sharply, Debbie might have been inclined to sit down without a fuss.

Such incidents are very typical and every teacher could describe the situations which are likely to result in conflict. As well as disputes over seating or moving seats, pupils will arrive late for lessons, fail to bring the right equipment or hand in work, talk when they should be attending and so on. As such contexts are so predictable it seems sensible to explore various ways of dealing with them in advance and role play can be extremely useful in this respect. It is important to remember that the object for the 'pupil' (in role) is not to win against the 'teacher' but to behave as the pupil would in such circumstances. I sometimes ask teachers to role play a seating dispute and on one occasion, a very satisfactory outcome was achieved. The dispute had begun when the 'teacher' entered and asked what the problem was. All three 'pupils' concerned bombarded her with their versions and continued to argue so the teacher gently took 'Debbie' aside and said 'I can see you're very upset about this Debbie. Would you just sit over there for five minutes as I've got to get the lesson started and then I'll come back and sort it out.' There are so many features in this brief statement which might have more general application. She acknowledged the pupil's feelings and took her plight seriously; her manner was calm and reasonable and the instruction was strongly mitigated; she offered a compromise, to sit 'for five minutes' and promised to try to find out the facts later, which would be seen as 'fair' treatment. She made her own concerns clear, to 'get the lesson started' and when this had been done the class would be occupied and the pupil might feel calmer.

Any predictable incident could either be role played or discussed by teachers in an attempt to learn better ways of coping. What does one do when a pupil refuses to pick up the litter (p.88), arrives when the lesson has started (p.96) makes a contemptuous remark (p.35) or fails to hand in homework (p.146)? In some cases it might even be possible to role play incidents which have occurred, using the people concerned but exchanging the teacher and pupil roles. This could be enlightening as each would be faced with a portrayal of himself, albeit probably exaggerated, and would have some experience of being in the other person's shoes. The process itself of trying mutually to find better solutions to conflicts would be quite therapeutic but it could only take place in a school where relationships were already cooperative. This latter point is quite crucial. In a school where relationships are cooperative and there is mutual respect between teachers and pupils, serious conflicts will be less likely to arise and easier to resolve to the satisfaction of both parties. This does not necessarily require informal relationships but a shared understanding of the particular authority agreement which exists.

7 The Way Ahead

It is surely in the interests of all concerned to promote cooperative relationships within schools. This does not mean that teachers should always concede to the demands of every pupil to avoid causing offence, but rather that they should share a common understanding of their respective roles. Classroom control does not depend upon dealing effectively with disruptive behaviour, but on providing an atmosphere and context in which cooperative relationships can develop. The questions are therefore how can teachers improve their skills in this respect and which systems of pastoral care are the most helpful?

A teacher's claim to authority rests largely on the capacity to teach effectively and there is clearly a need to develop ways in which they can be helped to improve their skills after the initial training. Most teachers learn new skills by acting on advice from more experienced colleagues, attending courses or simply from their own mistakes. After the probationary year the process is largely left to the initiative of individual teachers but with the recent introduction of school-based in-service training, there is now the opportunity for more collective and coherent staff development. Some schools have always arranged staff conferences, perhaps on a residential weekend, where the teachers meet in a relaxed atmosphere to discuss an agenda of their own choosing. If pupils could also be represented this would not only provide a valuable perspective but would help to develop a spirit of cooperation and responsibility. If relationships are to be improved both parties should be involved in the process; acting unilaterally is an expression of power which becomes increasingly untenable as pupils grow older.

Disruptive behaviour is frequently a source of stress and teachers should be able to discuss their problems with experienced colleagues before they become too serious. However, the following frank account written by a probationary teacher describes the problems she is experiencing and illustrates how difficult it is for others to offer practical assistance:

1 I have obviously not been strict enough from the beginning – a lesson always learned too late. My standards were not as high as they should have been, and I have not managed to nip trouble in the bud. Consequently, it has escalated, and many pupils have lost all respect for my authority.

2 I find it very hard to be consistent in dealing with problems that arise.

This is partly a case of routine and organisation, and getting the kids aware of (*i*) the limits, (*ii*) the punishments.

I have not made it clear enough what is and is not acceptable partly because every situation is different, so I tend to react differently. I find it hard to draw a clear line with respect to the issue of punishment. When is poor homework approaching the level of no homework? The crime is always very relative, and I am always acutely aware of what *is* and isn't fair – the kids constantly remind me of this.

3 I am far too compassionate, and forgive and forget too easily. This reflects my personality, which I am trying to change in the classroom. I can see their viewpoint too easily, and have become too familiar with many pupils before distancing myself enough to gain respect. I am also aware of lowering my personal standards for what I expect from the kids – most seem to have no manners at all, or else are blatantly rude, and one almost comes to expect this as the 'norm'.

4 I have 8×35 minute lessons free each week. Despite this, I find it increasingly difficult to prepare/evaluate work and mark books as I would like. I seem to put more work and effort into lessons than I receive from entire classes, and have become very disillusioned with many classes. I also spend more time chasing up pupils for detentions etc. than they spend doing the punishment. This results in my not always having the energy to 'perform' and 'act' in the class as I might wish.

5 I would like to illustrate some of these points with an example – L7 (1st year – 12-year-olds). This group I have taught since Christmas, prior to which they have been messed about with several science teachers. They are not an easy group, and I am by no means the only teacher who has trouble with them – they were hand-picked for nastiness from middle school records. There are about 10 prime trouble-makers (out of 29) – mixed-ability class. I began trying to be as unpleasant as possible by jumping on any misbehaviour, pulling out individuals, and making an example of them. I tried to vary the tone of my voice – waiting for them to shut up and calm down, and not shouting over them. This works, but is a very boring process. It may take them several minutes to calm down. I can then bawl at them whilst they are listening. As soon as I begin talking normally again, carrying on with the lesson, one or two individuals begin talking as I do – I stop, tell them off, and meanwhile, some others start. They take advantage of me talking to individuals to escalate the problem – soon lots of them are talking again, and we have to wait again for them to shut up. Each time this happens, we wait longer and longer for them to quieten down again. With all the stops and waiting, the better behaved pupils get bored, and they start messing about and talking too, saying how boring the lesson is.

The alternative seems to be to carry on regardless of a few people talking (which I have been advised against by everyone except the science adviser!) This would hopefully get enough people interested that the others would soon realise they were missing out on something, and listen. In practice, this does not work, and people cannot hear me because of others talking, and lose attention, or start shouting out. In science, this situation could be potentially very dangerous, and I am very reluctant to do practical work with this group, as half of them never listen to instructions. At the same time, I feel very sorry for the good pupils who are being held back. I have tried getting them to side against the unsociable members of the class, but the good kids then get beaten up as well!!

We have tried holding the whole class back for an hour's detention. This worked for a lesson or two afterwards, but has since lost its effect. The head of science has warned the lads that he will cane any more offenders, but again, I run into the problem of 'drawing the line', when so many are misbehaving in a gradual trend from mischief to hooliganism! What is a canable offence? What gets lines? Detention? etc.

It is surprising how frequently probationary teachers complain that they have been given some of the most difficult classes. If this is the case it is surely very unwise as there is then the greatest chance that they will fail to establish their authority and lose confidence. Senior staff and advisers will then have the problem of supporting them in their frequent conflicts with pupils in the full knowledge that a more experienced teacher would have handled the situation better. A new teacher is not only unusure of the routines and organisation of the school and preoccupied with planning and marking pupils' work but is also learning what it means for them to be 'the teacher'. This is very evident in the comments above (2), as there are obviously no hard and fast answers to the questions posed. She has to decide for herself in each situation what she can expect from the pupils and what they can expect from her. In short, she must quickly form her own definition of the situation (see Chapter 2). If she is undecided herself on these matters she cannot possibly expect the pupils to be clear about her position. The extent that one acts in accordance with any principle, stated or unstated, will reflect the strength of one's convictions, and it is from this basis that one can negotiate changes. The alternative, which has arisen for this teacher, is that the pupils express their own definition and from her account they seem unwilling to negotiate. From the outset the teacher has characterised the relationship with 'L7' as a battle, 'trying to be as unpleasant as possible' and in view of her inexperience it is not surprising that she is losing. It is inevitable that she has become emotionally involved with the group and talks of 'forgiving' and of their 'nastiness' but personalised feelings are not helpful in such situations. Pupils soon realise they have the power to please or upset the teacher which offers them a great deal of control in their interactions.

What can be done to help staff experiencing such problems? It might be possible to offer a fresh start with different classes but if one can observe at first hand what is actually happening one can give more specific advice. It is difficult for an experienced colleague to observe in the lessons because as soon as they enter, order is immediately restored and hence they may unwillingly take on a 'law enforcement' role as the only means of offering help. Unfortunately this can be extremely detrimental because the teacher may feel that his already limited authority is being overridden. Without witnessing what is happening in typical interactions with pupils, it is often impossible to identify exactly why situations develop as they do. So the headteacher, or senior member of staff, may spend a disproportionate amount of time dealing with the behaviour problems which arise with one or two teachers, but be unable to offer any advice on how they might avoid their problem in the future. It seems important that ways should be sought of overcoming the problem of how to observe classroom interaction without unduly affecting it.

Many schools now possess video recording equipment which provides the opportunity for teachers to record their lessons and discuss them later with other members of staff. The quality of the sound is far more important than the picture quality and the use of radio transmitter microphones either attached to the teacher's clothing or positioned around the room together with a multi-channel receiver are far superior to a simple camera microphone. If the school does not have this equipment, it may be possible to borrow some from a nearby college. Indeed, staff from colleges of education may be interested in helping as a form of in-service education, by recording lessons and joining in the subsequent discussions. Of course, such an open approach would require careful preparation if teachers who were the focus of the exercise were not to feel threatened. There must be a clear understanding that it is not the purpose of the observation to evaluate the professional competence of the teacher. Rather, the hope is that all participants, whether observers or observed, will learn from such an exercise.

Audio-tape recording of lessons can provide a useful record of one's teaching but the quality is often poor particularly when there is background noise from the pupils. It also lacks the additional visual cue showing who is speaking, available with video recordings. One can detect some of the major errors, such as failing to introduce a lesson adequately or talking above noise, but it is usually difficult to hear contributions from pupils unless they are close to the microphone. The extract concerning a pupil arriving late for a lesson (p.96) was recorded on audio-tape, with additional notes made at the time, but there was no background noise to obscure the speech. A major disadvantage is that one has no record of what may be quite crucial aspects of non-verbal behaviour.

When any form of recording is carried out, the pupils' behaviour can be affected if they are aware of what is happening, particularly when television cameras are being used. At the end of a science lesson being recorded with fourteen-year-olds, the pupils began to protest as the teacher gave out worksheets to do for homework. They argued that he didn't normally set homework, and one boy remarked that he had 'never used that thing before either', indicating the overhead projector on which the teacher had shown some beautifully prepared slides. 'It's because of that camera', they jeered, and one comedian added, 'Sir, why haven't you hit anyone today?' The longer one can have such equipment apparently in use in a room, the more likely it will be that pupils and teachers will become accustomed to its presence. It would be ideal if some schools were permanently equipped with unobtrusive recording facilities in at least one classroom, as good video recordings of normal classroom interactions are hard to come by and invaluable in training teachers.

Another possible way of overcoming the 'policeman' effect of senior staff in the classroom is for nearby schools to exchange staff at certain times during the week. Experienced teachers can then observe lessons and offer advice without directly affecting the behaviour of the pupils to any great extent, particularly if they avoid any interactions with pupils. A simpler method, suggested in Chapter 5, requires teachers to note down details of the events which occur during a lesson, so that these can form the basis for discussion with other members of staff. It is not always easy to be entirely objective when doing this, or to remember all the relevant details, but it is at least an approach which does not require any special equipment or outside observers.

I received the following account from a probationary teacher of chemistry which, from his final statement, I took to be a compendium of all the difficulties he had experienced. He later assured me that it was an account of one lesson and only the incident with the newt happened at another time.

> This is a fairly low ability second year class which has a double period of chemistry once per week, immediately after morning break. They are wild in the corridor. Line them up – girls on the left, boys on the right. They remain boisterous. Girls enter first and sit down. The boys swarm all over the room, which, being a biology laboratory, has side benches loaded with specimen cases, tanks of frog spawn, glass boxes of live beasts, and other distractions.

> 'Sit down please!'

> Getting everyone in place takes about seven minutes. During this time, gas taps are turned on; the skeleton in the metal locker is screamed at; brushes, pipettes, etc. have to be recovered.

> The boys are told to bring their stools and sit in front of the first bench for a demonstration. Three drag their heels, look out the window, and have to be cajoled – meanwhile three boxes of matches have been stolen from the end of the teacher's desk.

> Introduction is performed: interrupted by requests to go to the toilet. Tina feels sick; are we going to use the bunsens, and so on. Demonstrate the setting up of the apparatus, and how to heat the boiling tube. The class are now restless – 'Can we start now?' First back to places, and

reinforce the method by labelling a diagram from a handout booklet.

Some girls scream. The locusts are crawling over the floor. The bung has been removed from their box. Chase the creatures and get them back in the case. While this distraction was going on several bunsens have been lit, and there is a smell of burning rubber. X is heating the rubber tubing. All the bunsens are extinguished. Apparatus is collected from cupboards.

No-one seems to be assembling their apparatus properly. Move around helping. Those helped first heat their tubes too strongly, and in the wrong places. 'X is on fire'; Y – 'the tubing has come off'. 'Sir, Derek has broken a thermometer and hid it in a drawer'. 'What is all this broken glass on the floor?' N has broken his apparatus. 'Sir, Derek has thrown a beaker out of the window.'

Collect in the apparatus. Write notes on the experiment on the board, and the class copies them down. 'Sir, David has swallowed a live newt!' 'Take him to Mr Y.'

This gives you the flavour of many of my classes. The school has apparently a policy of giving the most disruptive low ability class to probationers.

There are clearly several points where the teacher should not have continued with the lesson, starting from when the class were waiting 'wild in the corridor' and an alternative action can be discussed. There is also a need to establish safe procedures in the laboratory and the teacher needed to make a more fundamental examination of his role.

The opportunity to watch experienced teachers is one which many students take advantage of, and there is no reason why such arrangements should not be made with staff in a school. Observing how successful teachers cope in their first meetings with difficult classes can be very helpful, provided the observer knows what to look for. Whether one is observer or observed, it is important to be able to identify the variables crucial in the development of an interaction. It is frequently argued that teachers differ in the ways they achieve discipline, but in recent years research and observation has demonstrated that they also have a great deal in common. Wragg *et al.* produced a booklet for use on teaching practice listing seven areas to which students' attention was drawn. These were personal relationships, preparation and planning, beginnings and endings (of lessons), transitions, appropriateness (of work undertaken), vigilance (akin to 'withitness') and clarity (of presentation). The students were expected to work in pairs, with the help of school staff and college tutors, so that each could act as observer for the other's lessons. This is an excellent idea because student observers carry less authority than class teachers, but can still provide useful feedback as well as learning from the experience. Gnagey (1975) reviewed research on effective classroom discipline and derived a checklist of procedures which teachers could use to assess their own disciplinary techniques. There has, however, as yet been little attempt to include the ways in which a teacher's non-verbal behaviour can influence the result of interactions.

The general school ethos has an effect on the type of relationships which teachers develop with their pupils. There are limits to the extent that one can behave informally in a school which is run on very formal lines and vice-versa. What may be particularly important is the way disputes with pupils are officially treated within a school, as Galloway *et al.* (1982) concluded.

> The 'official channels' often seemed to carry a built-in escalation clause. If you were going to seek help or support from a colleague, you sought it from a senior colleague, at least at middle management level. In turn this led to a related problem. First it created a climate in which teachers felt they could refer a pupil *to* a colleague, with the implication – which the colleague often resented – that she would investigate and deal with the problem. This seemed to contrast with the climate in other schools which encouraged teachers to discuss problem pupils *with* colleagues, with the implication that the teacher might be able to deal with it herself. A logical result was that relatively minor issues could escalate from a dispute between a subject teacher and pupil to a confrontation between the head and the pupil, culminating in exclusion or suspension.

Galloway goes on to suggest that this devalued the role of the form tutor in playing an important part in the pupils' pastoral care.

In cases where teachers and pupils are unable to resolve their disputes to their mutual satisfaction, a system which refers the problem upwards in the staff hierarchy emphasises the 'power' aspect of the relationship, and senior teachers become the heavy artillery called upon when teachers are losing battles. In a system where the problem is considered to be in the *relationship*, both parties would consult a counsellor or conciliator and teachers might be less inclined to characterise their relationships with pupils as being based on power. There is a great deal of evidence to suggest that positive attitudes towards pupils are associated with fewer discipline problems. For example, 'deviance insulative' teachers (Hargreaves, 1975) were optimistic and assumed pupils would behave and cooperate. They liked and respected all pupils and enjoyed meeting them outside the classroom. Similarly, Reynolds and Sullivan (1981) found that the 'crucial factor' distinguishing schools which had an 'incorporative' rather than a 'coercive' approach to pupils was the 'perceptions amongst teachers'.

> In schools which have adopted a coercive strategy, there is a consistent tendency to *over-estimate* the proportion of pupils whose backgrounds can be said to be 'socially deprived' ... and to under-estimate their pupils' ability.

The way disputes are dealt with in a school will reflect, and to some extent determine, the attitudes and relationships which develop between teachers and pupils and among the staff themselves. It is not within the scope of this book to examine the systems which schools operate but if one is concerned with developing cooperative relationships, the implications go beyond the individual teachers. They may also go beyond the school as it is not uncommon for teachers to find themselves dealing with a spate of unwanted behaviour and attitudes which were presented the evening before on television.

In conclusion, it may be helpful to summarise some of the features of classroom interaction and practice which are significant in teacher-pupil relationships. The checklist is not presented as a dogmatic set of instructions to be followed at all times. Teaching situations differ considerably and an observer might use the list flexibly to focus on aspects of lesson content and organisation, teacher self-presentation and classroom management skills. These are clearly interrelated and over-lapping areas which will be evident from an examination of the factors listed under each heading in the checklist.

Checklist for successful teaching

1   Teaching is more likely to be successful if:
    - lessons have an overall theme. Aims should be considered and one's teaching should have continuity;
    - each lesson has specific objectives;
    - work is thoroughly prepared (p.69);
    - the choice of work is appropriate to the age and ability of the pupils;
    - the work makes intellectual demands on the pupils (p.94);
    - pupils are sometimes expected to work in silence (p.100);
    - marking is regular and thorough (p.92);
    - the form of presentation and the activities undertaken are varied;
    - the seating and layout of the classroom is appropriate to the activity (p.17).

2   When teaching, the pupils' attention can be better sustained by:
    - standing prominently in the room (p.69);
    - engaging in eye contact with individual pupils (pp.66–8);
    - demonstrating one's involvement with the subject: enhancing the meaning with vocal variations reinforced by bodily move-ments and facial expressions (pp.61–6);
    - looking for and responding to feedback from pupils (p.72);
    - moving closer to those who do not appear to be attending (p.16).

3   The momentum and smoothness of the lesson will be improved by:
    - ensuring a prompt and brisk start (p.96);
    - introducing the main theme clearly. Avoid dealing with side issues, unnecessary repetition of points already understood and interrupting one's teaching with lengthy reprimands or justifica-tions of one's action (pp.95–7);
    - ensuring there are no noticeable breaks in the lesson which

could have been avoided (pp.97–100);
- not attending to individuals or small groups at the expense of the whole class (p.95);
- allowing time to conclude the lesson in an organised and orderly manner (p.96).

Such measures reduce the opportunities for pupils to misbehave. Reasoning and justification of one's actions should take place at times set aside for the purpose, rather than providing pupils with an alternative to work.

4   Questioning is more likely to increase motivation and conceptual development if:
- the questions are intriguing and thought provoking and require pupils to reflect on their views and observations (p.104);
- pupils are encouraged to express their views and opinions openly as they will then be more inclined to justify them (p.104);
- the questions are not asked as if they are tests (p.102);
- the teacher asks follow-up questions, involves other pupils, sometimes withholds answers and acts as devil's advocate (p.104);
- all answers are treated as acceptable and, if appropriate, as valuable (p.102).

5   Questioning can give rise to management problems in large groups if:
- the answers require some time for thought and are given at length (p.103);
- the teacher does not indicate clearly who 'has the floor' or forgets to call on those who wish to contribute (p.105);
- the teacher fails to ask short factual questions with pace or directs them to only a few pupils. They should be used to keep a group alert and accountable and to check understanding (p.103);
- the teacher does not ensure that everyone attends to the answers given (p.105).

If questions are used appropriately, pupils are more likely to attend or participate actively than if they were simply expected to listen. However, if such sessions are not properly managed they can become noisy and uncontrolled and the teacher is then faced with restoring order. If the teacher is trying to promote small group discussion other strategies may be called for (p.105).

6   Confidence in one's authority will be expressed by:
- using pupil's territory, personal space and property in a relaxed, non-threatening manner (pp.12–18);
- standing prominently in the room (p.69);
- avoiding tension in body posture, facial expression and voice (pp.3–7, 90);

- maintaining eye contact with pupils in a relaxed way (when not talking) (pp.26–31);
- controlling one's own responses (pp.31–5):
  - not answering or giving eye contact to those who call out,
  - choosing not to return smiles,
  - resisting interruptions or dealing effectively with them,
- ensuring that the pupils respond to the teacher in some way (p.35).

Such measures contribute to the impression that one's authority is legitimate and are helpful when trying to create a controlled and attentive atmosphere in which to teach.

7 Forceful, dominant behaviour expresses personal power in a relationship and is conveyed by:
- moving into the pupil's personal space (p.15);
- bodily facing the pupil (p.11);
- staring at the pupil with a menacing expression (p.26);
- towering over the pupil (p.15);
- using commands in a threatening tone of voice (p.55);
- not moving when speaking (p.71);
- raising one's voice (p.56).

Such behaviour towards pupils may result in hostile compliance or an emotional confrontation (pp.34, 139).

8 A teacher will be less likely to contribute to unwanted behaviour by:
- not following it with rewarding attention (pp.82–3);
- discouraging peer group attention (pp.84–5);
- avoiding an emotional outburst (pp.86–7, 90);
- making it easier and more rewarding for pupils to do the work set than to avoid it (pp.90–4).

9 To lessen the coercive connotations of reprimands and hence appeal to the pupils to cooperate, they can be mitigated by:
- addressing them anonymously to the whole group (p.112);
- delivering them quietly or privately to individuals (p.112);
- using 'please', a polite tone of voice and relaxed manner (p.111);
- phrasing them as questions, though not with a pleading tone of voice (pp.112–16).

In some formal schools direct imperatives are normally used and express the hierarchical nature of the relationship (p.45).

10 Reprimands or instructions which interrupt pupils' activities carry more impact if:
- they are given only when really necessary (pp.56, 122);
- contact is achieved before the message is given: pupils should be silent and attentive (pp.56–8);
- they are brief and as clear as possible (pp.113–15);
- they are phrased as clear directives (p.117);

- bodily movements are limited when speaking (p.71);
- speech is delivered in a 'measured' tone (p.71);
- the pupil is lightly held by the upper arm or shoulder (pp.19–26). (**NB** Male teachers, particularly at the secondary level should avoid touching girls (p.22). *If there is any suggestion of aggression or force, or if one's authority is in question, touching is likely to escalate the conflict rapidly.* (p.22).)

Unmitigated reprimands may be perceived as an expression of the teacher's claim to power and can lead to confrontations.

11 Reprimands and punishments are more likely to suppress unwanted behaviour if they:
- interrupt the behaviour as early as possible (p.117);
- are consistently applied and enforced. Threats should be backed up (p.121);
- are sufficiently disagreeable to discourage future misbehaviour (p.120);
- deal with the offence rather than the offender. Do not personalise reprimands (p.122);
- there is an alternative, legitimate way for the pupil to achieve the same goal (p.124).

12 Confrontations and disputes with pupils are more likely to be resolved successfully for both teacher and pupil if:
- a cooperative relationship already exists (p. 141);
- they are not carried on publicly (p.139);
- the teacher does not use dominant, threatening behaviour (p.139);
- respect is shown towards the pupil (p.140);
- the pupil's feelings are acknowledged (p.142);
- a compromise can be offered (p.138);
- a calm atmosphere is maintained (p.139). Any anger shown should only express one's concern for the pupils not one's attempt to intimidate them;
- the tension can be relieved with genuine humour (p.140).

After any dispute normal relationships should be re-established as soon as possible without appearing to ingratiate oneself (p.140).

It is preferable that aversive treatment should be used as negative reinforcement for desirable behaviour rather than as punishment to suppress unwanted behaviour (p.119). Reprimands and punishments are most effective in establishing that a teacher means what he says, but are of less use in retrieving situations which are out of hand, as pupils have by then learned to disregard them. They play a limited role in establishing control compared with the techniques of good management and efficient teaching. However, matters of discipline should be discussed among staff and, where appropriate, senior pupils, in order to agree on procedures in relation to unwanted behaviour.

These discussions may also decide upon official ways of acknowledging desirable behaviour and work, such as letters to parents or personal congratulations from the headteacher. In this way, rules and demands for work can be seen as part of a general school policy and not merely as whims of individual teachers.

This book has been teacher-centred, not in an attempt to put pupils in their place, but because, even when faced with motivational and intellectual deficiencies in the child and an adverse environment, it is the teacher's responsibility to see that children learn.

Good classroom control and good teaching go hand in hand. It might be possible, though highly undesirable, to teach indifferently and still maintain control, but without control good teaching can never begin. Central to this whole process is the nature of the authority claimed by teachers and the extent to which it is based on effective and caring teaching. The final word in this respect is left to a fourth-year girl describing her feelings about some of her teachers:

> If they tried to enjoy it I think, if they tried to enjoy teaching us, um, everyone would be better for it because they, they're thinking, 'Oh Gawd not again!', you know. And if you ask them, 'Excuse me can you explain it again?', they think 'Oh Gawd we've got a right one 'ere' and er, they think 'Why should I enjoy it?' and er, 'I've got to do it. It's a job', and they don't enjoy it.
>
> So we can't enjoy it either.

References

ARGYLE, M. (1975) *Bodily Communication*, Methuen.

ARGYLE, M. and COOK, M. (1976) *Gaze and Mutual Gaze*, Cambridge University Press.

ARONFREED, J. (1968) *Conduct and Conscience*, Academic Press.

ARONFREED, J., CUTLICK, R. A., and FAGAN, S. A. (1963) 'Cognitive structure, punishment and nurturance in the experimental inductions of self-criticism', *Child Development*, **34**, 281–94.

AUSUBEL, D. P. (1968) *Educational Psychology: A Cognitive View*, Holt, Rinehart and Winston.

BALL, S. J. (1980) 'Initial Encounters in the Classroom and the Process of Establishment' in WOODS, P. (ed.) *Pupil Strategies*, Croom Helm.

BARNES, D., BRITTON, J. and ROSEN, H. (1969) *Language, the learner and the school*, Penguin.

BIEHLER, R. F. (1978) *Psychology Applied to Teaching*, 3rd edn, Houghton Mifflin.

BRAZIL, D. (1976) 'The Teacher's Use of Intonation', *Educational Review*, **28**, 180–9.

BRODEN, R. M. (1971) 'The effects of self-recording on the classroom behaviour of two eighth grade students', *Journal of Applied Behaviour Analysis*, **4**, 277–85.

BROWN, G. A. and EDMONDSON, R. (1984) 'Asking Questions' in WRAGG, E. C. *Classroom Teaching Skills*, Croom Helm.

BRUCE, D. (1973) 'Language and Cognition', *Cambridge Journal of Education*, **3**, 1, 2–11.

BUZAN, T. (1971) *Speed Memory*, David & Charles.

CHEYNE, J. A. and WALTERS, R. H. (1970) 'Punishment and Prohibition' in CRAIK, K. (ed.), *New Directions in Psychology 4*, Holt, Rinehart and Winston.

CONDON, W. S. (1976) 'An Analysis of Behavioural Organisation', *Sign Language Studies*, **13**, 285–318.

COOK, J. (1975) 'Easing behaviour problems', *Special Education: Forward Trends*, **2**, 1, 15–17.

COULBY, D. and HARPER, T. (1985) *Preventing Classroom Disruption*, Croom Helm.

DANZIGER, K. (1976) *Interpersonal Communication*, Pergamon.

DAVIES, B. (1983) 'The Role Pupils Play in the Social Construction of Classroom Order', *British Journal of Sociology of Education*, **4**, 1, 55–69.

DEPARTMENT OF EDUCATION AND SCIENCE (1978) *Truancy and behaviour problems in some urban schools*, HMSO.

EXLINE, R. V. (1972) 'Visual Interaction: The Glances of Power and Preference'. *Nebraska Symposium on Motivation*, pp.163–206 University of Lincoln Press.

EXLINE, R. V. and YELLIN, A. (1969) 'Eye contact as a sign between man and monkey' Symposium on non-verbal communication, Nineteenth International Congress of Psychology, London, reported in Exline *op cit.*

FESTINGER, L. (1961) 'The psychological effects of insufficient rewards', *American Psychologist,* **16,** 1–11.

FLANDERS, N. A. (1968) 'Interaction analysis and inservice training', *Journal of Experimental Education,* **37,** 126–32.

FRANCIS, P. (1975) *Beyond Control?,* Allen and Unwin.

FRENCH, P. J. and PESKETT, R. (1986) 'Control Instructions in the Infant Classroom', *Educational Research,* **28,** 3, 210–19.

FURLONG, V. (1976) 'Interaction Sets in the Classroom: Towards a Study of Pupil Knowledge', in STUBBS, M. and DELAMONT, S. *op. cit.*

GALLOWAY, C. M. (1979) 'Teaching and Non-Verbal Behaviour' in AARON WOLFGANG (ed.) *Non-Verbal Behaviour: Applications and Cultural Implications,* Academic Press.

GALLOWAY, D., BALL, T., BLOOMFIELD, D. and SEYD, R. (1982) *Schools and disruptive pupils.* Longman.

GANNAWAY, H. (1976) 'Making Sense of School', in STUBBS, M. and DELAMONT, S. *op. cit.*

GILLHAM, B. (ed.) (1981) *Problem Behaviour in the Secondary School,* Croom Helm.

GLASSER. W. (1969) *Schools Without Failure,* Harper and Row.

GNAGEY, W. J. (1960) 'Effects on classmates of a deviant student's power and response to a teacher-exerted control technique', *Journal of Educational Psychology,* **51,** 1–9.

GNAGEY, W. J. (1975) *Maintaining Discipline in Classroom Instruction,* Macmillan.

GOFFMAN, E. (1959) *Presentation of Self in Everyday Life,* Penguin.

GRAY, F. (1974) 'Little Brother is Changing You', *Psychology Today* (March).

HALL, R. V., AXELROD, S., FOUNDOPOULOS, M., SHELLMAN, J., CAMPBELL, R. A. and CRANSTON, S. (1971) 'The effective use of punishments to modify behaviour in the classroom', *Educational Technology,* **11,** 4, 24–6.

HAMBLIN, R. L., BUCKHOLDT, D., FERRITOR, D., KOZLOFF, M. and BLACKWELL, L. (1971) *The Humanisation Processes,* John Wiley and Sons.

HARGREAVES, D. H. (1967) *Social Relations in a Secondary School,* Routledge and Kegan Paul.

HARGREAVES, D. H. (1972) *Interpersonal Relations and Education,* Routledge and Kegan Paul.

HARGREAVES, D. H. (1984) 'Teachers' Questions: open, closed and half-open', *Educational Research,* **26,** 1, 46–51.

HARGREAVES, D. H., HESTER, S. K. and MELLOR, F. J. (1975) *Deviance in Classrooms,* Routledge and Kegan Paul.

HARRIS, C. S., THACKRAY, R. I. and SCHOENBERGER, R. W. (1966) 'Blink rate as a function of induced muscular tension and manifest anxiety', *Perceptual Motor Skills,* **22,** 155–60.

HARROP, A. (1974) 'A behavioural workshop for the management of classroom problems', *British Journal of In-Service Education,* **1,** 1, 47–50.

HOLMES, J. (1983) 'The structures of teachers' directives' in RICHARDS, J. C. and SCHMIDT, R. W. (eds) *Language and Communication,* Longman.

HOWELL, S. (1981) 'Rules not Words' in HEELAS, P. and LOCK, A. (eds) *Indigenous Psychologies,* Academic Press.

KENDON, A. (1967) 'Some functions of gaze-direction in social interaction', *Acta Psychologica,* **26,** 22–47.

KENDON, A. (1972) 'Some relationships between Body Motion and Speech' in SIEGMAN, A. W. and POPE, B. *Studies in Dyadic Communication*, Pergamon.

KENDON, A. (1983) 'Gesture and Speech: How they Interact' in WIEMANN, J. M. and HARRISON, R. P., *Non-verbal Interaction*, Sage Publications.

KILBURN, J. (1978) 'Better for Both – thoughts on teacher-pupil interaction', *Education 3–13*, **6**, 2, 9–11.

KOUNIN, J. S. (1970) *Discipline and Group Management in Classrooms*, Holt, Rinehart and Winston.

KOUNIN, J. S. and OBRADOVIC, S. (1968) 'Managing emotionally disturbed children in regular classrooms: a replication and extension', *The Journal of Special Education*, **2**, 2, 129–35.

LASLETT, R. and SMITH (1984) *Effective Classroom Management*, Croom Helm.

LEPPER, M. R., GREENE, D. and NISBETT, R. E. (1973) 'Undermining children's intrinsic interest with extrinsic reward: A test of the "over justification" hypothesis', *Journal of Personality and Social Psychology*, **28**, 129–37.

MCNAMARA, E. and HEARD, C. (1976) 'Self-control through self-recording', *Special Education: Forward Trends*, **3**, 2, 21–30.

MAHONEY, M. J. and THORENSEN, C. E. (1972) 'Behavioural self-control – Power to the Person', *Educational Researcher*, **1**, 5–7.

MARLAND, M. (1975) *The Craft of the Classroom: a Survival Guide*, Heinemann Educational Books.

MEDNICK, S. A., GABRIELLI, W. F. and HUTCHINGS, B. (1987) 'Genetic Factors in the etiology of crime' in MEDNICK, S. A., MOFFITT, T. E. and STACK, S. A. *The Causes of Crime*, Cambridge University Press.

MEHRABIAN, A. (1972) *Non-verbal Communication*, Aldine Atherton.

MILLS, I. (1975) 'Can the human brain cope?' *New Scientist* (16th October 138–40).

NEILL, S. R. ST. J. (1987) *Non-verbal Communication – Implications for Teachers* in MARTINSSON, B. G. (ed.) *On Communication*, 4 (SIC 13), University of Linköping.

NEILL, S. R. ST. J. (1988) 'Non-verbal Communication – its signficance for the Pastoral Specialist', *Pastoral Care in Education*, **6**, 7–14.

O'LEARY, K. D., KAUFMAN, K. F., KASS, R. E. and DRABMAN, R. S. (1970) 'The effects of loud and soft reprimands on the behaviour of disruptive students', *Exceptional Children*, **37** (October) 145–55.

PARTINGTON, J. A. and HINCHLIFFE, G. (1979) 'Some aspects of classroom management', *British Journal of Teacher Education*, **5**, 3, 231–41.

PIK, R. (1981) 'Confrontation Situations and Teacher-support Systems' in GILLHAM, B. *op. cit.*

PRESSLAND, J. (1978) 'Behaviour modification – theory and practice', *Education 3–13*, **6**, 1, 43–6.

REYNOLDS, D. and SULLIVAN, M. (1981) 'The Effects of School: A Radical Faith', Re-stated in GILLHAM, B. *op. cit.*

ROSENBURG, H. (1976) 'Modifying teachers' behaviour', *Special Education: Forward Trends*, **3**, 2, 8–9.

ROSENSHINE, B. (1970) 'Enthusiastic teaching: a research review', *School Review*, **78**, 4, 499–514.

ROSS, A. (1978) 'The lecture theatre is a world of entertainment', *Times Educational Supplement* (23 June).

RUTTER, M., MAUGHAN, B., MORTIMORE, P. and OUSTON, J. (1979) *Fifteen Thousand Hours*, Open Books.

RYAN, K. (1970) *Don't Smile 'till Christmas*, Chicago Press.

SKINNER, B. F. (1971) *Beyond Freedom and Dignity*, Penguin.

SMITH, H. A. (1979) 'Non-verbal communication in teaching', *Review of Educational Research*, **49**, 4, 631–72.

SOLOMON, R. L. (1964) 'Punishment', *American Psychologist*, **19**, 4, 239–52.

SPADY, G. (1973) 'Authority, Conflict and Teacher Effectiveness', *Educational Researcher*, **2**, 4–10.

STRONGMAN, K. T. and CHAMPNESS, B. G. (1968) 'Dominance hierarchies and conflict in eye contact', *Acta Psychologica*, **28**, 376–86.

STUBBS, M. (1976) 'Keeping in Touch: Some Functions of Teacher-talk', in STUBBS, M. and DELAMONT, S., *op. cit.*

STUBBS, M. and DELAMONT, S. (1976) *Explorations in Classroom Observation*, John Wiley and Sons.

TANNER, L. N. (1978) *Classroom Discipline for Effective Teaching and Learning*, Holt Rinehart and Winston.

TATTUM, D. (1982) *Disruptive Pupils in Schools and Units*, Wiley.

THOMAS, A., CHESS, S. and BIRCH, H. G. (1968) *Temperament and Behaviour Disorders in Children*, New York University Press.

THOMAS, W. I. (1931) *The Unadjusted Girl*, Little Brown & Co.

TORODE, B. (1976) 'Teachers' Talk and Classroom Discipline', in STUBBS, M. and DELAMONT, S., *op. cit.*

TURNER, B. (1973) *Discipline in Schools*, Ward Lock Educational.

WADD, K. (1973) 'Classroom Power in Discipline in Schools', in TURNER, B. *op. cit.*

WATSON, O. M. and GRAVES, T. D. (1966) 'Quantitative research in proxemic behaviour', *American Anthropology*, **68**, 971–85.

WEBER, M. (1958) in GERTH, N. and MILL, C. W. (eds) *Essays in Sociology*, Oxford University Press.

WEINRAUB, M. and PUTNEY, E. (1978) 'The effects of height on infants' social responses to unfamiliar persons', *Child Development*, **49**, 3, 598–603.

WEITZ, S. (1974) *Non-verbal Communication*, Oxford University Press.

WHELDALL, K., BEVAN, K. and SHORTALL, K. (1986) 'A Touch of Reinforcement: the effects of contingent teacher touch on the classroom behaviour of young children', *Educational Review*, **38**, 3, 207–16.

WHELDALL, K. and LAM, Y. Y. (1987) 'Rows versus tables II. The Effects of Classroom Seating Arrangements on Classroom Disruption Rate, On-task Behaviour and Teacher Behaviour in Three Special School Classes', *Education Psychology*, **7**, 4, 303–12.

WHITE, R. and BROCKING, D. (1983) *Tales out of School*, Routledge and Kegan Paul.

WILSON, M. and EVANS, M. (1980) *Education for Disturbed Pupils*, Schools Council Project Working Paper 62, Eyre Methuen.

WOOD, P. and SCHWARTZ, B. (1977) *How to get your children to do what you want them to do*, Prentice-Hall.

WRAGG, E. C. (1981) *Class Management and Control: A Teaching Skills Workbook*, Macmillan.

WRAGG, E. C. (ed.) (1984) *Classroom Teaching Skills*, Croom Helm.

WRAGG, E. C. and WOOD, E. K. (1984a) 'Teachers' First Encounters with their Classes' in WRAGG, E. C. *op. cit.*

WRAGG, E. C. and WOOD, E. K. (1984b) 'Pupils Appraisals of Teaching' in WRAGG, E. C. *op. cit.*

WRIGHT, D. (1973) 'The Punishment of Children', in TURNER, B. *op. cit.*